arcocolourcollection

interior design

Interiors

interior design

Author
Francisco Asensio Cerver

Publishing Director
Paco Asensio

Proofreading
Tobias Willett

Graphic Design
Mireia Casanovas Soley, Quim Serra Catafau

ISBN: 84-8185-015-2 (complete collection)
84-8185-019-5 (Interiors)

Interiors

The universe of interior design constitutes an ambiguous field of research which can be approached from numerous perspectives. In fact, the relationship between the individual and his immediate space constitutes a reality as old as mankind, and which can be interpreted in as many ways as there are.

In reference to the more technical aspects of interior design, it is necessary to emphasise the most frequently used systems of distribution and spatial organisation. Differences in levels are still maintained, but the introduction of platforms or levels in interiors with a pronounced vertical tendency serve to illustrate new systems of volumetric division. These structures are usually located over bathrooms, kitchens and junk rooms, with the object of allowing the areas of common activity to enjoy more extensive vertical perspectives and a greater sense of space.

The other great innovation in distribution schemes is the negation of the conventional role of walls and panels in the separation of spaces; this supposes a resounding victory for the concept of the loft. Physical barriers pose visual restrictions and diminish the qualitative values of the most expressive aspects of these containers.

However, there is not an absolute disappearance of walls since in some family homes they are still indispensable for privacy.

It is necessary to highlight the relevance that one-room houses are acquiring in the activities of modern urban life. The rejection of this type of space in previous decades has given way to a necessary alternative for the lifestyles of individuals or couples who prefer a nomadic existence.

All the works which make up this volume can be placed within one or other of the currents we have outlined but this cataloguing is never of an absolute nature. The tendencies overlap and are superimposed, and the homes appear as eclectic combinations in which, nonetheless, there can always be observed an attitude which stands out over the rest.

We must first make reference to the old industrial buildings which have been recently restored and put to domestic use.

Another kind of building is constituted by the barn, and, in a sphere closer to the urban context, the enormous buildings of bygone times are undergoing processes of restructuring and division aimed at bringing them closer to the methods of modern life.

All in all, the projects in this volume are no more than samples of a heterogeneous and plural creative process in which the evolution of economic and social structures has as much importance as the cultural and existential philosophies. However, the most essential part of interior design is its definition of the home as an abstract mental space, the reflection of personal experiences and sensations.

Interiors

Interior design

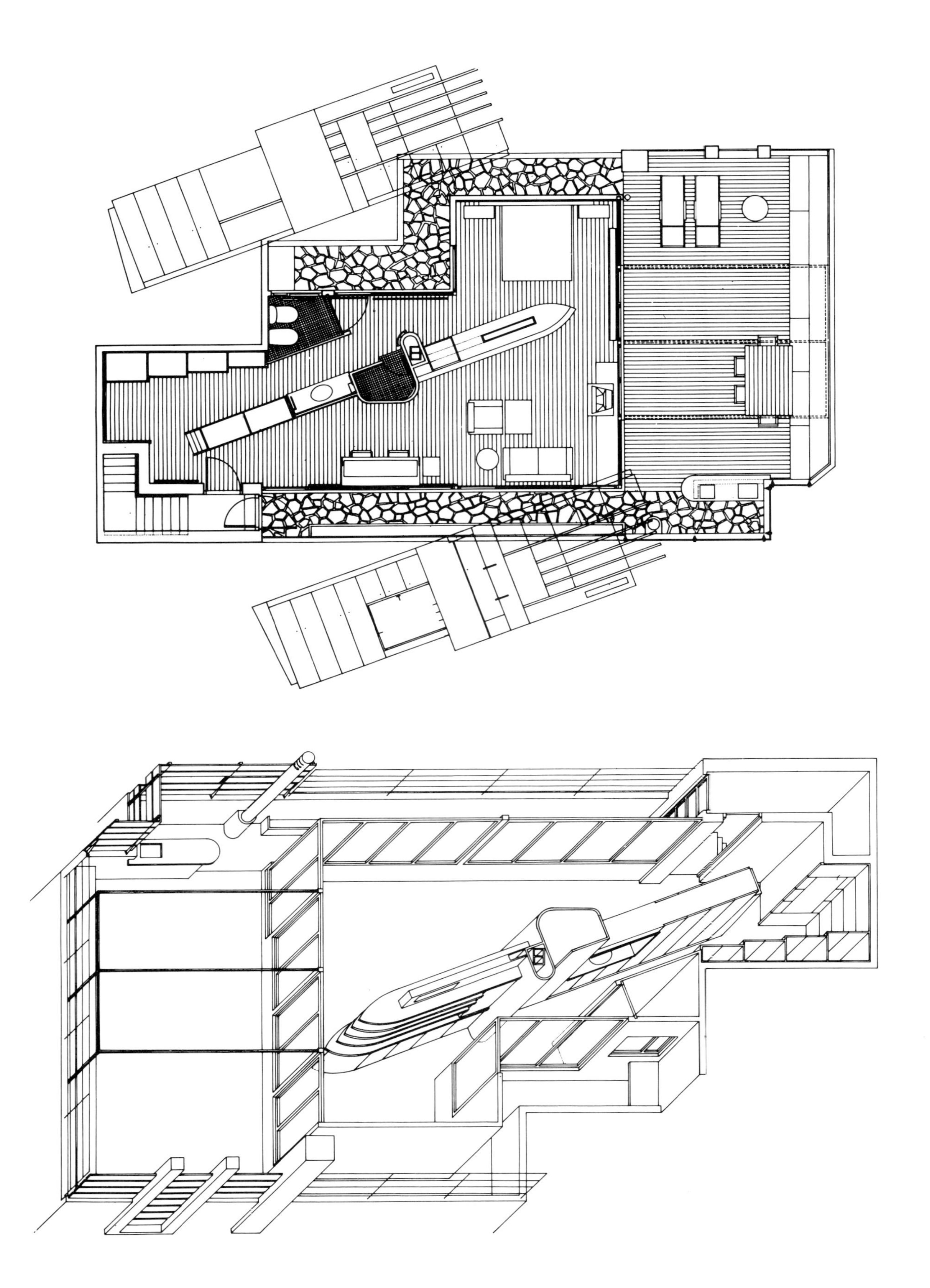

General plan of the house.

Axonometric plan.

Private residence

Josep Boncompte & Guillermo Font

The project for the adaptation of an interior as living space proposed by Josep Boncompte and Guillermo Font was selected for the 1989 FAD awards in the field of interior design. The execution of the work began in November of 1988 and was completed in May of the following year. The building is situated on the Carrer Sant Gervasi de Cassoles in Barcelona, and its penthouse serves as a complementary living space for the flat below. The original floor plan was a highly irregular composition formed by asymmetrically joined rectangles. The largest of these rectangular surfaces is the terrace, which almost completely surrounds the living space.

The objective of the interior plan was to order the two different areas, the flat and the terrace, both considered as complementary elements. The interior distribution was guided by the potential for the natural lighting of the rooms offered by the elevated position, and the terrace was adapted to fulfill new needs as outdoor, usable rooms.

The original structure was crossed by a ventilation flue, adding a further problem to the irregularity of the floor plan. A rigid permanent division offered no solution to the conflicts. A bold, innovative plan was needed that would articulate the rooms and relate them to a central motif.

The solution proposed consisted of a free-standing architectural element that would enclose the flue, at an oblique position in relation to the exterior walls. The area would remain a unified space with no strict divisions, but with an appropriate room distribution that represents a break with conventional composition. Compartmentalizing the

This module divides the space in two parts.

The closets of the bedroom gradually increase in volume to make use of the space created by the inclination.

A wooden stairway on a metal structure communicates the two levels.

Partial view of the dining room area.

interior through an inflexible arrangement of partitions would not have overcome the obstacles that stemmed from the irregularity of the floor plan. Furthermore, the complementary function of the penthouse with regard to the flat below it defined its programme; it was to serve as a suite.

The diagonal structural element is thus the articulate and ordering axis of the space. A natural itinerary through the new floor begins on the floor below. A wooden stairway on a metal structure communicates the two levels. The entrance to the penthouse consists of an irregular hall in which the distributing component offers two possible itineraries. The logical route leads the visitors first to a kind office with a volume that gradually increases due to the obliqueness of the central element. The greatest breadth is found in the living room. Although this is a unified space, a clear functional differentiation is apparent. Both the living room and the office enjoy the natural light offered by the continuous openings in the partitions that forms a glazed gallery when the terrace is reached.

Off the living room is a bedroom accommodated by one of the larger regular rectangles, which offers an impression of spaciousness. This room receives natural light from the large windows overlooking the terrace that are placed above a low wall. The central architectural element also serves as an extension of the bathroom, enclosing the washstand and a medicine cabinet. Along its length, a distributing nucleus also contains closets that supplement those built into the opposite partition. The closets gradually increase in volume to make use of the space created by the inclination.

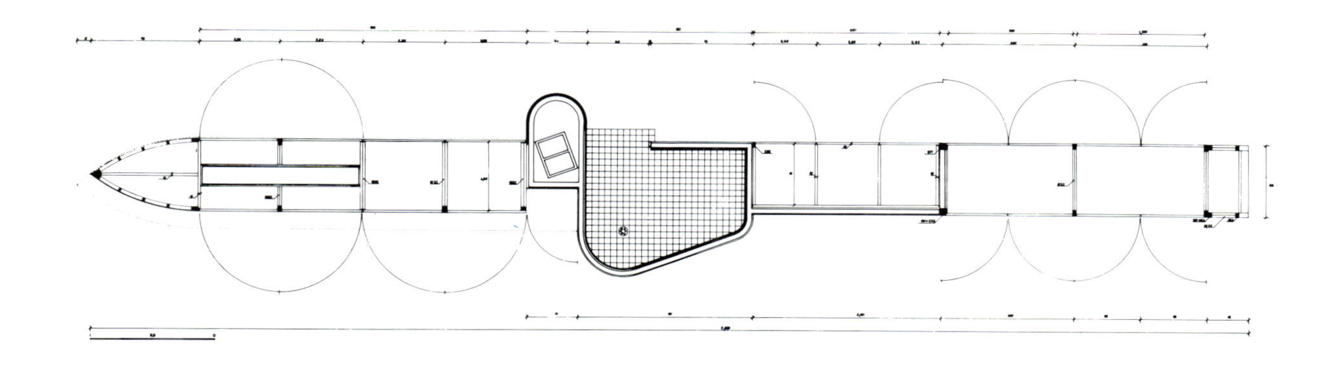

One of the corners of the house.

Wood is the essential material employed in the rectangular leisure area.

Once the interior was planned, the architects turned to the structuring of the terrace to adapt it to the new programme. The irregular original floor plan was formed by a rectangle that grew from its shorter ends and thus defined the layout of the living space. To distribute the outdoor area, its functions were divided. The largest section is the terrace as such, an area for rest and relaxation, and the second area provides access to the household facilities, such as the washing machine.

The floor of the terraces is developed as a regular rectangle covered by a sloping canvas awning that screens the area from the higher buildings nearby. The perimeter of the sun deck is demarcated by a wooden fence supported by bars and metal trellises concealed by climbing plants. The greenery is of great importance to

The main bedroom from the terrace.

Partial view of the living room.

Detail of the bathroom.

the composition and marks the limits of the outdoor area.

The interior designer, Blanca Tey de Salvador, collaborated on the finishes of the house and the terrace. The original volume was characterised by a light structure and aluminium window and door frames. Wood is now the dominant material, used for the flooring as well as for the fabric of the closets and furniture. The central distributing nucleus, in its role as a container, is also of wood. Its masonry structure exposed behind the five wooden platforms serving as shelves determinated this free-standing element in the form of a keel.

Small blue tiles are used in the bathroom facilities in the central structure to cover the sheathing of the ventilation flue. Metal towel racks are set into the cylindrical volume of the flue. The washstand area is finished in marble and glass. As a whole, the interior decoration is based on the chromatic interplay of various types of wood, on the arrangement of ornamental and functional details around the central structure, and on the skilful placement of the windows that provide natural light.

The decoration of the terrace is based on the difference in floorings and the treatment of the furniture. Wood is the essential material employed in the rectangular leisure area. Most of the section around the penthouse is paved in stone.

Through a uniquely effective structural strategy, the planners distributed the space with partitions, positioning rooms that are barely suggested in relation to a new conception of the terrace, which is independent and, at the same time, complements the indoor living space.

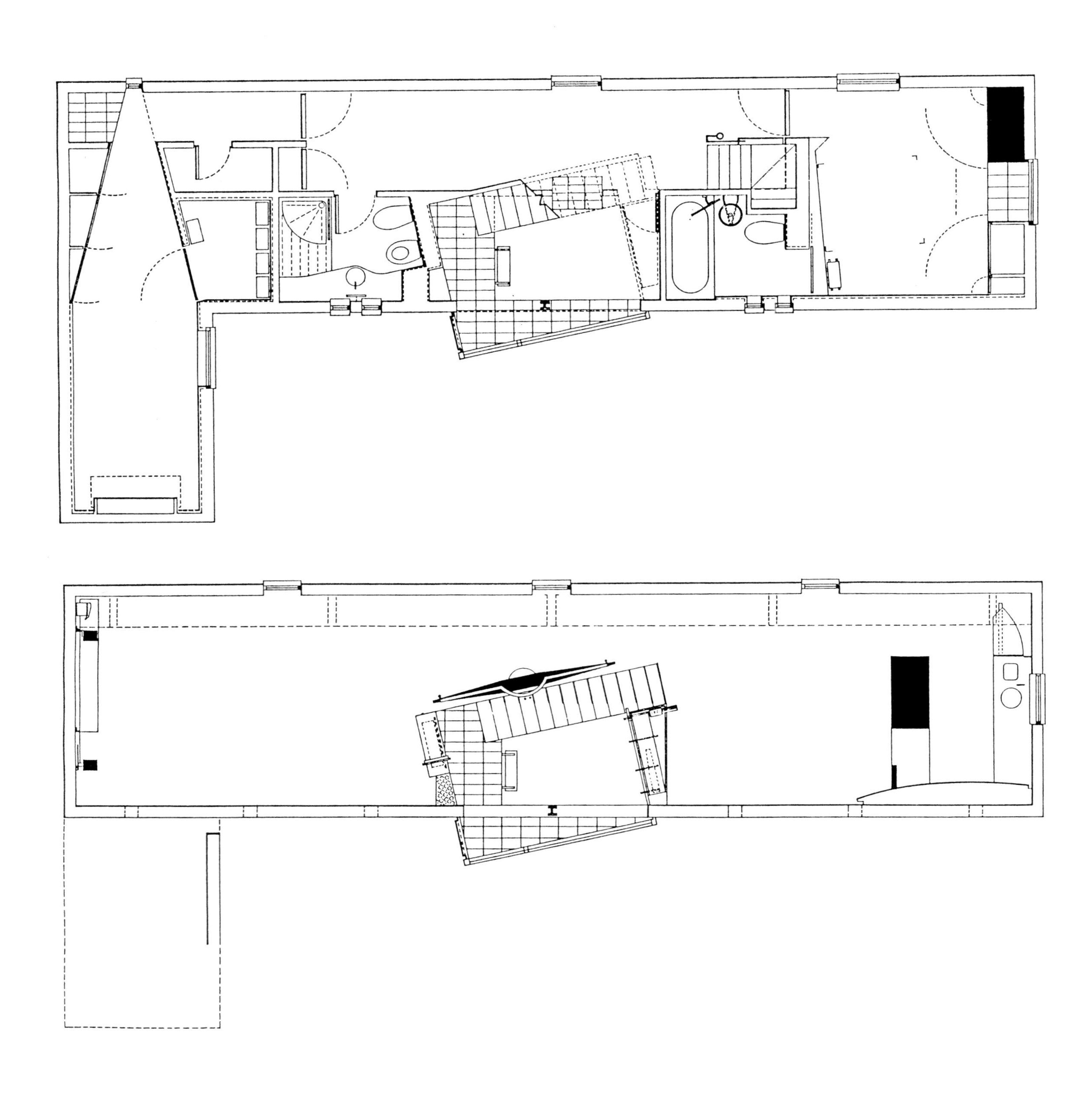

Plan of the ground floor.

Plan of the upper floor.

Blackburn House

Peter Wilson

Blackburn House represents the triumph of tenacity over the frustrating limitations on creative, revolutionary construction in England and, more specifically, in an urban setting such as London. Thanks to the understanding of open-minded clients and to favourable planning conditions, the studio formed by Peter Wilson, Julia Bolles-Wilson and Eberhard Klefner successfully completed an exceptional work, whose siting on the streets of the British capital would have been difficult. The structure is an expressive and plastic architectural exercise and, at the same time, a delicate and subtle interior design.

The architects remodelled several old structures of scant aesthetic value, adding a new volumetry that departed in both form and function from the original buildings. According to Wilson himself, the project represents a rejection of the established canons, serving as a pause, an interruption in the urban context of contemporary society. To achieve this end the building was envisioned as an autonomous object, as an independent mass to serve as a point of reference and as a link. This conception was the basis for the planning of Blackburn House. Without representing an obvious intrusion in the urban setting, this combined office and residence illustrates a profusion of contemporary, inventive ideas, particularly on themes concerning the architectural process and the internal programme. This study will be focused on these points, but not without a previous description of the setting that influenced the planning.

Lateral cross section.

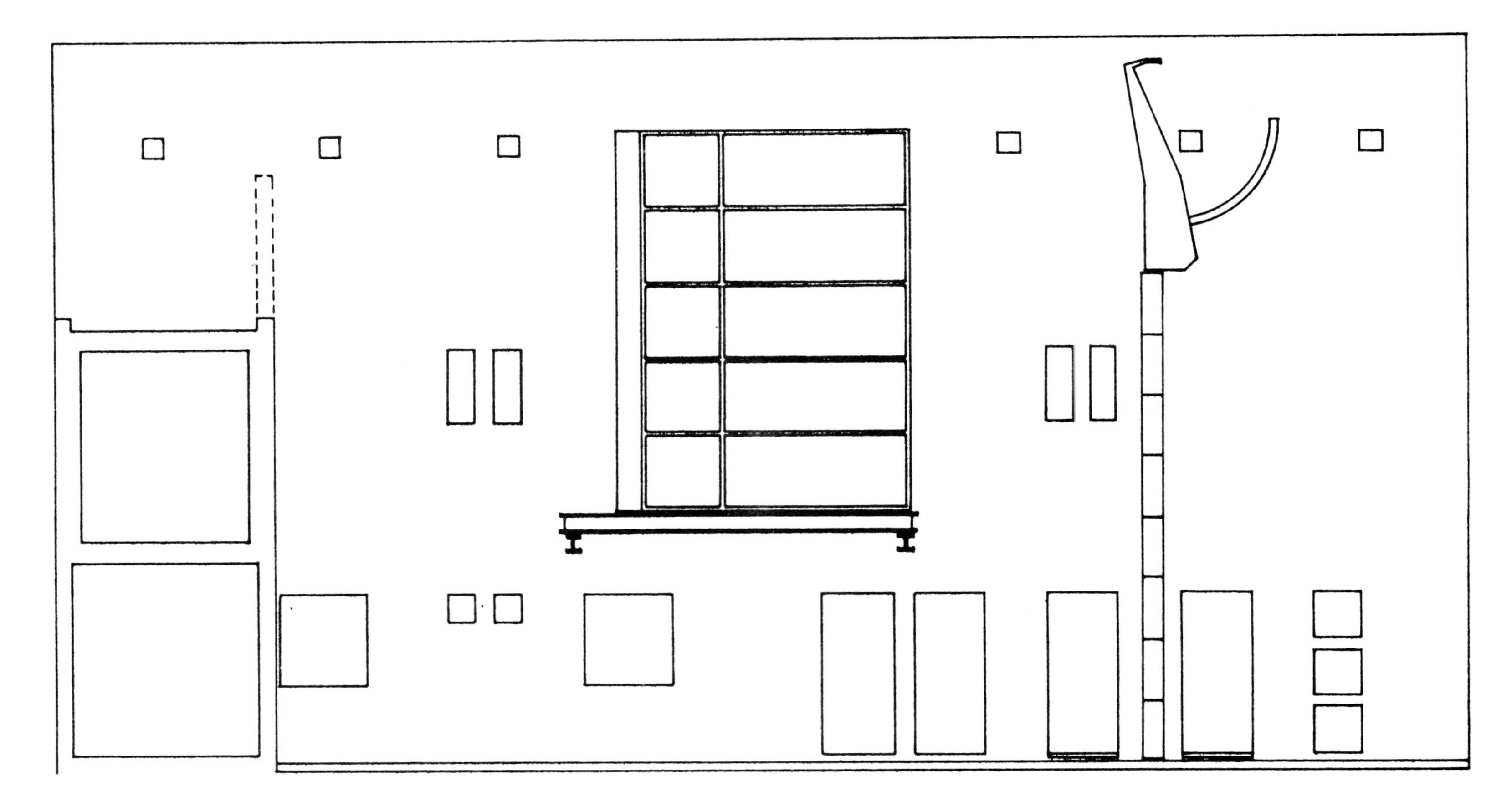

As mentioned above, the likelihood of constructing a modern, ambitious piece of architecture in present-day London is very remote. Only the open minds of the clients (David and Janice Blackburn) and, most important, the ideal site of the project made its execution possible. However, the relativity of the benefits of the site should be borne in mind, since its only advantage is that it is not visible from the street. This factor allowed the architects complete creative freedom and, with the blessing of the owners, they were able to execute a work that is as unusual as it is attractive.

The intervention involved the restructuring of a group of existing stables that freed a space which had no visual connection with the streets. Within it a new architectural volume could be designed with no typological or legal constraints. The project was planned in accordance with Wilson's theories, completely independent from the context, in an attempt to create an isolated structure with its own meaning and values.

The architectural composition was centred exclusively on the two aspects of volume and facade. The first involved completing the original unfinished structure of the stables, at the same time gaining the required space. Regarding the second aspect, much time and energy was devoted to planning the facade in accordance with two basic principles. The first was the complete expressive freedom already noted and the second was the shielding of the occupants and the contents from the indifferent visual sequences of the surrounding buildings. With these singular objectives, the conventional sense of the facade *was reinterpreted, since the goal in this case was not to show or suggest the interior with respect to the setting, but the opposite: to safeguard and protect that interior.*

Because of its siting, a single facade was planned for the building, and on its surface the entire expressive content of the design would be concentrated. This was determined by the lack of multiple perspectives, a result of its position; only one side of the building is exposed. The basic volume was supplemented by a perpendicular module with a pitched roof, which increased the usable space, screened the main facade from public view and created a small, closed internal street. The entrance to the interior of the building is through this additional structure.

The plasticity of the main elevation is generated by two elements of remarkable fabric, which combine an imaginative aesthetic with utilitarianism. Both provide a compelling contrast to the extreme whiteness of the overall surface and the necessary visual tension in the whole. Secondly, these elements represent attempts to offer a practical solution to the functional problems arising from the indifferent surroundings. The characteristics of these two elements merit a more detailed analysis.

The first is a huge window that emerges halfway up the facade. It extends obliquely across the entire front, initiating an interplay of planes, orientations and convergences that are remarkably effective. The visual effect is reinforced by two external beams that appear to

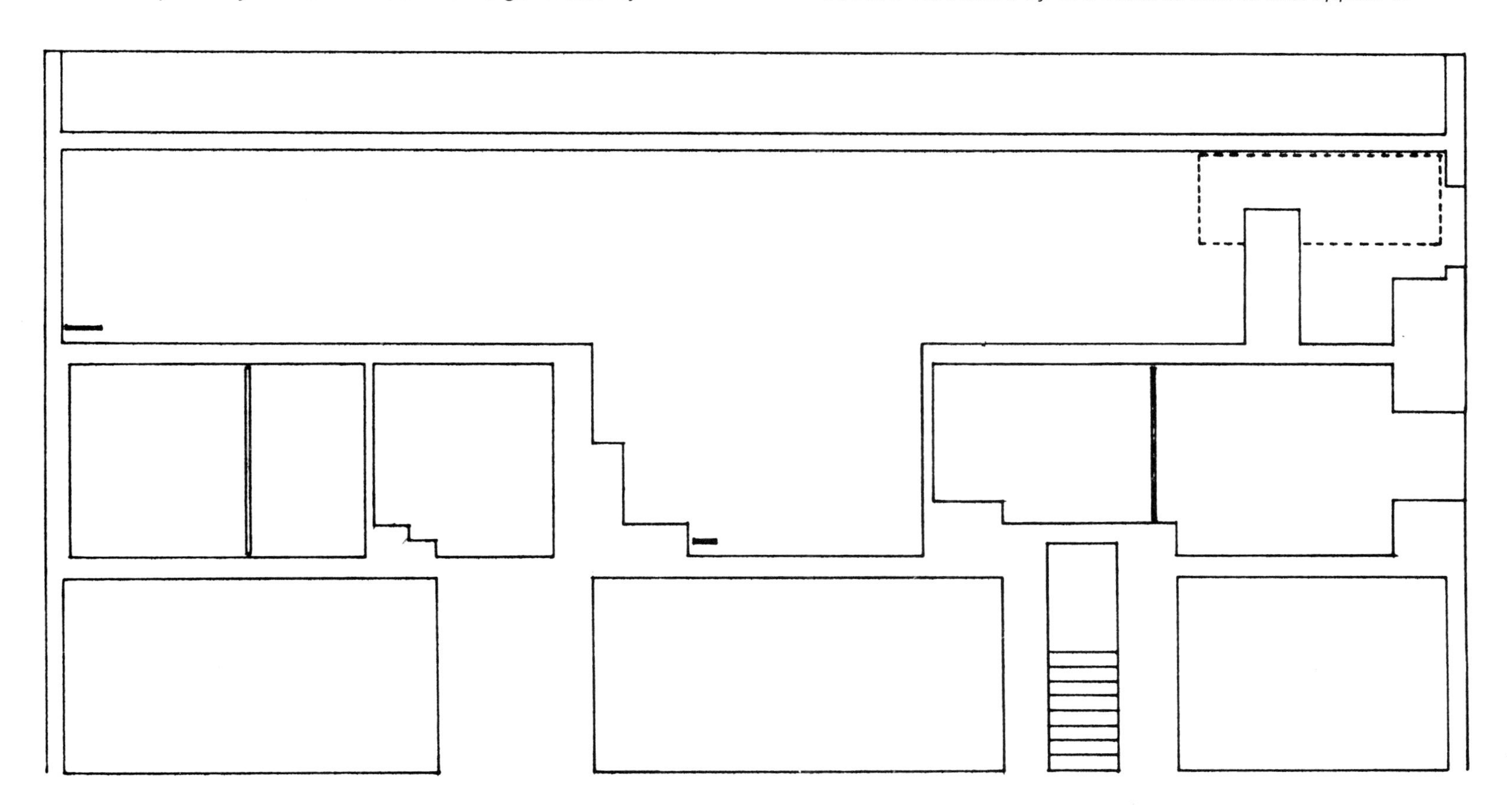

Cross section.

support the projecting structure of the window. The surface is executed in opaque glass (as are the rest of the windows) containing several transparent pieces, whose abstract lines form a subtle link between the interior and the exterior. The blind material was used to shield the house from the unattractive setting, while the stylized transparent sections, in addition to creating a plastic formal pattern, allow the interior to breathe visually. In this way, the window loses its conventional values and becomes its own opposite, a denial of its most characteristic function. In addition to the protection from the cityscape offered by this facade, a chromatic effect is achieved by the green copper doors on the lower section of the white surface.

The vast window shares the surface of the facade with a second element, partially sculptural, partially architectural, serving both aesthetic and functional purposes. The structure, known as the Totem, is built against the facade and consists of a column executed in welded plastic and stainless steel, an ironic reference to exterior piping that also plays a functional role: to pipe clean water into the house and eject the waste. Aesthetically it reinforces the vertical perspective to the building, while it also carries out one of the conventional processes of the domestic programme.

The programme is distributed on the three floors of the building. The ground floor accommodates the offices and the two upper storeys constitute the living space.

Converging walls train the eye towards the slit window, with its glimpse of the exterior.

The delicately furnished main corridor, showing the protruding steps of the oblique staircase that rises from the adjoining room.

A corner of the upper floor, with simple bench seating running along the wall.

The oblique room and staircase mark the transition between the two levels.

The second major achievement of the project is the interior architecture, a compendium of the most ingenious systems of spatial organization and interior decor. Each of the blocks is independent, but also interrelated within the overall context of the volumetric configuration, resulting in a single reality of undeniable expressive and conceptual value.

The perpendicular module, mentioned above, that forms the entrance to the building communicates with the first floor of the residence. This section contains an additional study with converging walls panelled in different types of wood. The rest of the apartment is defined by a longitudinal development on two floors, articulated by an empty space which corresponds in both volume and orientation to the vast oblique window of the facade. All of the rooms are distributed around this interior atrium, which links all the perspectives physically and visually.

The first floor contains the more private rooms (the master bedroom, the toilets and the storeroom adjoining the study). This was conceived as a transitional area between the surrounding city and the basic nucleus of the design – the top floor – where the occupants are completely insulated from the urban context. The communications system between these two storeys is a staircase of light, airy design. On the upper level the secluded ambience is related to the exterior only by the transparent fragments in the opaque glass and by a skylight that runs the length of the rear of the roof. Most of the collective household activities take place in this area. There are no structural barriers; the rooms (the

The bannister rail not only incorporates a seat but performs a compositional function, punctuating the upper floor.

View across the upper floor. Natural light pours in through the plate glass windows of the oblique room and the half concealed skylights that run the length of the building.

Detail of the bathroom. The coolness of the grey tiling and the metal fittings is offset by the mellow colour of the wood panelling.

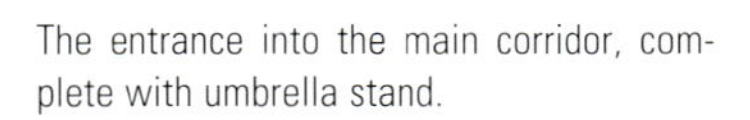

The entrance into the main corridor, complete with umbrella stand.

Textured metal plate is a recurring feature of the fittings.

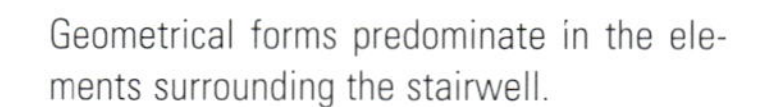

Geometrical forms predominate in the elements surrounding the stairwell.

living room, the dining room and the communicating kitchen) are ordered on either side of the central space. The back wall is left free for the display of paintings.

The inclusion of the most ambitious designs in furniture and decor constituted a danger to the harmony of the interior. The diversity of artists and styles (Barry Flanagan's hare, Scott Burton's chair, Andy Warhol's portrait, Bruce McLean's and Ron Arad's tables and Jasper Morrison's sofas) and the special attention given to the microdesign, could have brought about a fragmentation of the living space. But in spite of the fact that each of these pieces has an autonomous narrative, they are all similar in tone, and disruption was avoided by limiting the selection of materials and by a monochrome treatment. The nature of the decorative elements lies somewhere between architecture and sculpture. This is most apparent in the door furniture, the support column and the projecting platform (all in steel), the vitrine, the stylized table for the hi-fidelity system and, most arresting of all, the seat in the central atrium, whose sinuous form seems to float in the interior.

In this project the firm headed by Peter Wilson has executed a masterly combination of exterior and interior architecture from both the conceptual and aesthetic standpoints. Conceptually the work represents a triumph over the rigid, archaic urban building tradition, although to accomplish this the structure had to be concealed from public view. On the facade, all of the most conventional themes have been violated (for example, the glass protects rather than displays) through the use of

View of the upper floor from the dining area; straight lines alternate with subtle curves.

plastic and highly dramatic elements. In the interior, partitions were rejected in favour of the two-storey open space as the articulator of the rooms. Finally the iconoclastic designs in decor and furnishings define a way of life and an atmosphere that is completely isolated from the external environment. The concept of the autonomous, independent object governs both the interior and the exterior, safe from any type of constraint the modern city might impose.

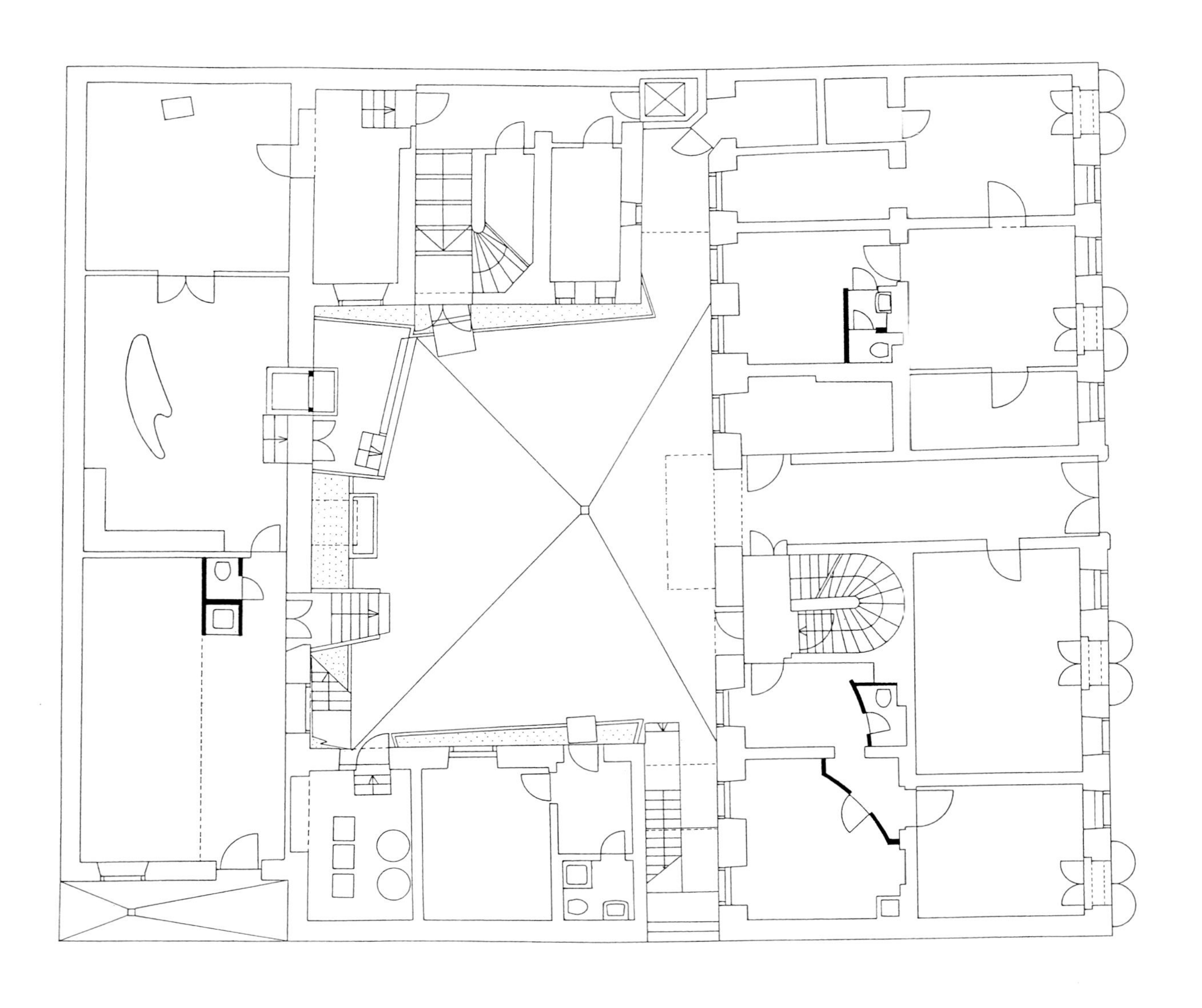

Floor plan.

Hermanngasse 29

Gertraud Auer & Rüdiger Lainer

The project undertaken by Rüdiger Lainer and Gertraud Auer at 29 Hermanngasse in Vienna touches on some of the burning questions of present-day housing design: the renovation of old buildings, the importance of architectural elements inside the domestic space, the difficult relationship between architect and client, and the individualisation and personalisation of lived-in environments. However, these two young Austrian architects have confronted the difficult task using original, markedly conceptual criteria which establish an unusual dialogue between the old and the new and between conservation and intervention. Lainer and Auer's proposal managed to overcome all the anticipated difficulties thanks to a complete agreement between intentions and results which can be summed up as the identification of the occupant with his or her environment, despite the variety of the functional programme.

The general project consisted of the renovation of two old structures, a sober office building from 1825 which gives onto Hermanngasse and a four-storey factory from the end of the XIX century, situated at the rear and separated from it by a small courtyard. The facade of the older building had to be preserved in accordance with the rules governing the renovation of historic buildings. Having been abandoned for many years, the complex had a desolate air and was structurally fragile, making the renovation work difficult.

Before the planning studies were made and the present owners acquired the property, it had been offered to other companies and groups interested in its

Floor plan.

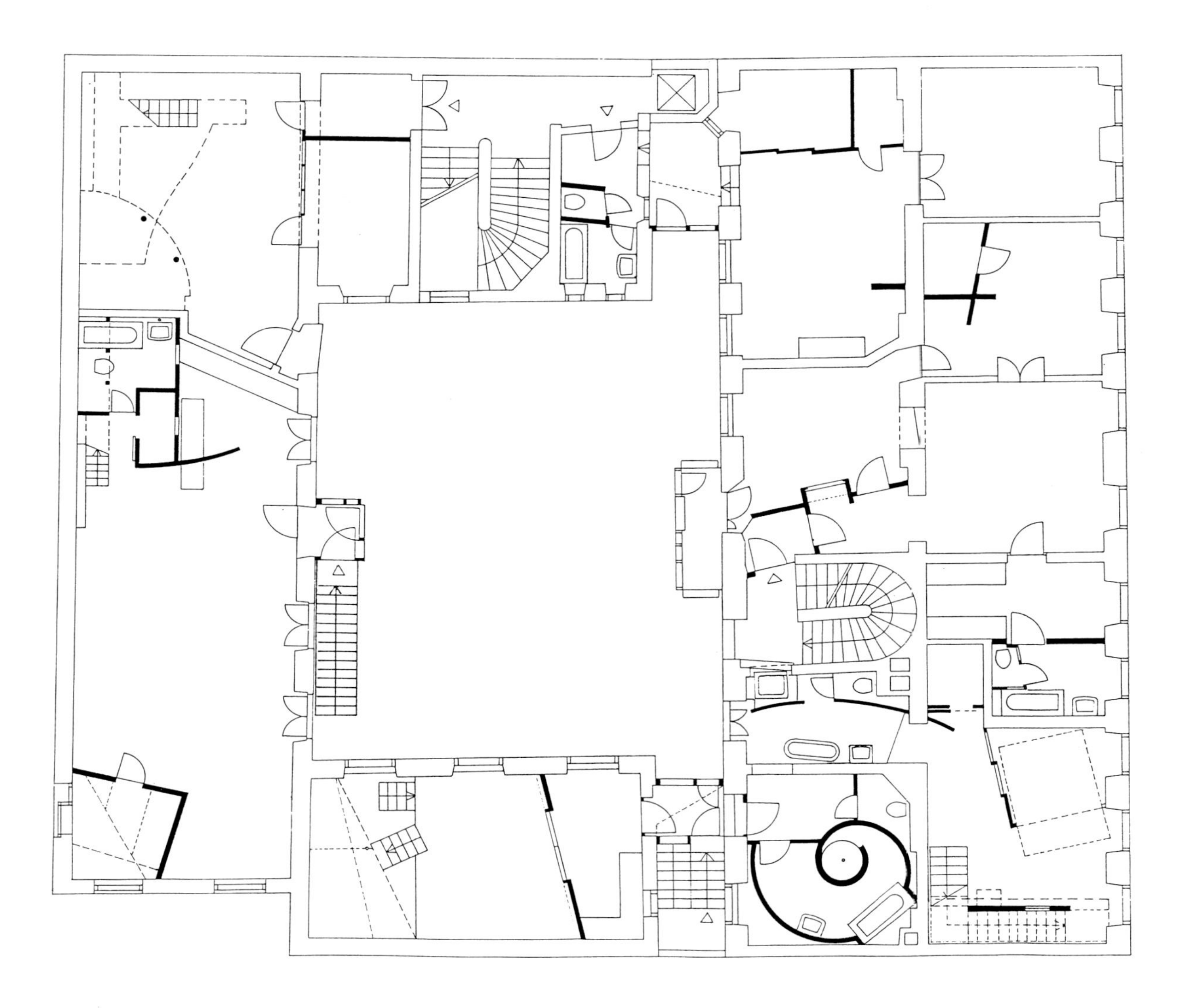

renovation and use. However, they finally abandoned the idea in the face of the difficulties which it presented and the costs involved. In order to overcome these initial contradictions, the project had to be based on the involvement of the future residents of the building and comply with the conditions of the Public Housing Development Act. With all these factors in mind, Lainer and Auer planned their intervention according to criteria of personal action which resulted in this new complex.

The two buildings have been converted into a block of thirteen apartments, a doctor's surgery, storage spaces and various leisure areas, which occupy an area of 1,550 m². Volumetrically the two blocks have been joined by a series of communicating bridges which convert them into a unitary reality. Given the impossibility of changing the eighteenth-century facade in Hermanngasse, the redesign of the exterior was limited to the placing of these connecting nexus and the replacing of the roof of the factory building, which was in a poor state of repair. The vivid colour of this new component, which acts as a terrace-garden, contributes to the animation of the building's image and displays on the exterior the complex restructuring which has taken place inside.

The key part of the project is the new group of apartments. The design of the domestic spaces presented multiple problems, given the need to combine the usual functional demands with the necessity to create numerous differentiated and autonomous living areas. The objective was not to create a single environment acceptable for a family of a single person, but to produce

Floor plan.

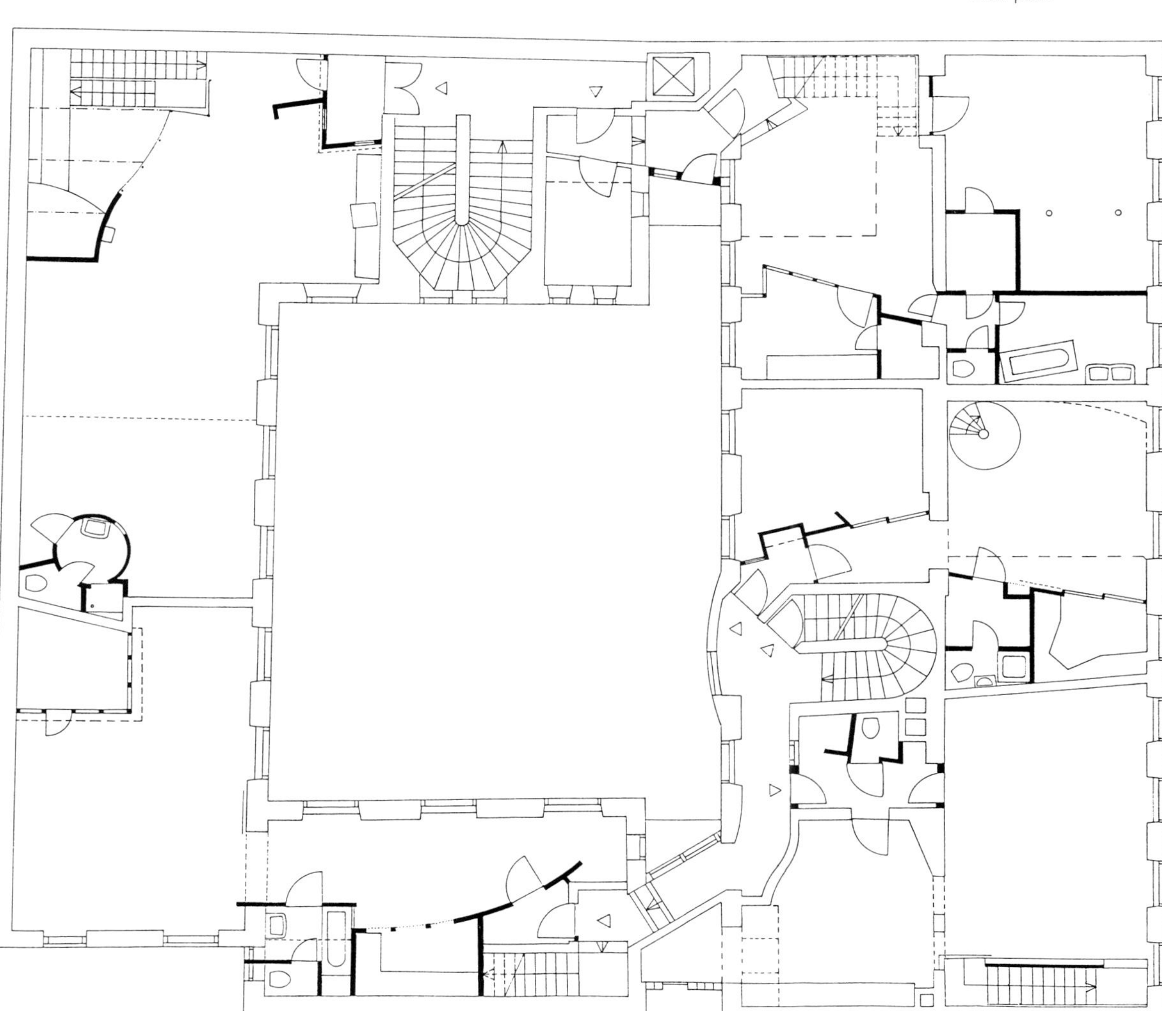

thirteen interiors which, despite having a certain uniformity through a homogeneous atmosphere and treatment, had to fulfil the requirements of individualisation in each specific case. Without exactly being social housing, the project touched on some of the most acute problems in this area of architecture, and faced the planners with the urgent necessity of creating spaces with formal independence as a reflection of lived experience.

Through a process of consultation between the architects and the future occupants, a conceptual agreement was reached: the apartments would be considered as an expression of the imagination and ideas of the occupant, displayed in metaphors and analogies which would be translated into formal solutions materialising the poetic and political capacities of the occupant. This almost spiritual dimension given to housing, and the ideological agreement between the architects and the clients constitutes a new vision of the possibilities of designing domestic space which in no way ignores the essential parameters of functionality and economy, or the creative urges of the architects.

Some general principles were used in the organisation of the internal volumetry which were designed to establish a close interrelation between geometry and scale: on the one hand, the connection of the new apartments with the heterogeneous urban framework and, on the other, the dialogue between the modern intervention and the old structures. The first responded to a formal criteria (the need for light, perspective and space) while the second was more spiritual (a play of

Floor plan.

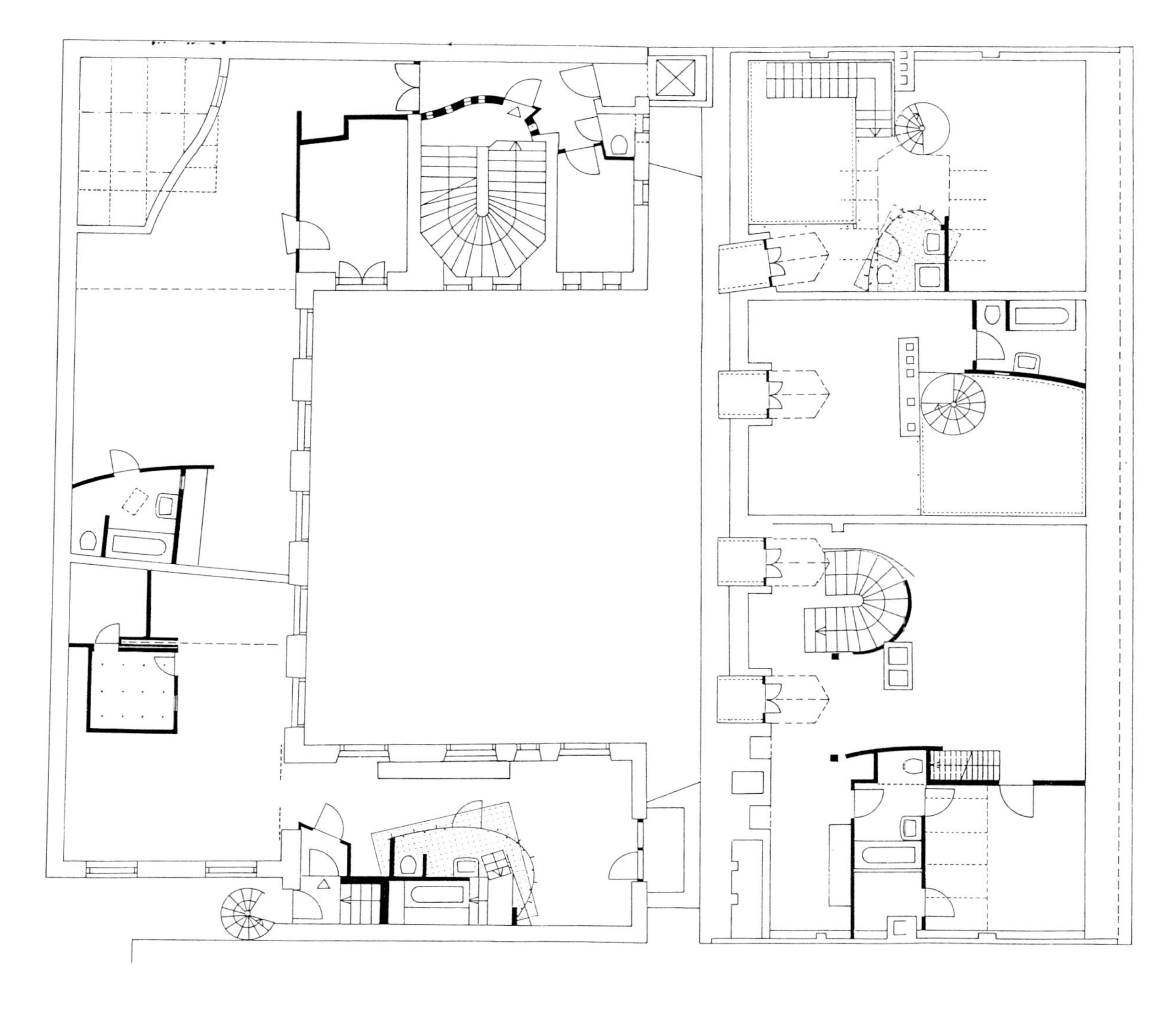

contrasts, despite a respect for the history of the building, not without a certain amount of irony). However, in practice, the objectives complemented each other in creating a unitary environment which was the essence of the project.

In relation to the first, the overall configuration of the two blocks favoured a division of the planned apartments between an appropriate number of openings, either to the exterior or to the interior. The resulting sections, distributed on one or two levels, were conceived as living spaces in accordance with the needs of contemporary families disposed to a reduction in the number of children, meaning that large areas with numerous rooms give way to smaller interiors which still respect the ratio of space to individual.

With regard to the relationship between the original container and the new internal organisation, the chief object has been to maintain the essence of the building as much as possible, integrating its structures (taking into account the needs of conservation) into the general concept of the project. The ironic element in this dialogue is present in the use of some damaged parts in old structure such as, for example, roofs in bad repair which have been used as skylights to good atmospheric effect.

However, the most decisive achievements of this type in the design relate to the importing of architecture into the interior, using elements which appear to emerge from the structural framework itself and are converted into central and identifying elements of the apartments. The relation between the new and the old is organised so that

Cross section.

the original building becomes a pre-existing box or container which does not lose its history and which, at the same time, takes in a series of architectural objects or fragments.

These fragments are important in a number of ways: in their capacity to generate the distribution and movement in each space, in their power to individualise each apartment, and in the enormous aesthetic potential of their finishes. The expression of their new specific uses is based on their position, form and in the choice of materials. A detailed account of the thirteen apartments would be of little use but some of the most representative and distinctive examples of the group can be analysed, after describing the properties common to all.

The characteristic which gives the distinct contents a unified atmosphere is the consistently light treatment of the walls, the warmth of the wooden flooring, the minimalist conception of the decoration and the transparent luminosity. In the general context some recurrent features can also be noted, such as the use of free planes (lightly curved and with intense colouring to enhance the visual impact), tucked stairways which give a light weightless connection between the levels, platforms which are often strangely shaped and placed. The materials used are, in the main, industrial or what are normally considered poor. Here, however, they are dignified and ennobled by the techniques of combination, superimposition and confrontation.

Apartment number eight is one of the few duplexes in the group. It has two singular features: the method of

The bold decoration brings out all the atmospheric potential of the winding staircase.

Form and colour combine to create soft features on the building's many curved surfaces.

delimiting the master bedroom, an unusual, wooden garage door system with textile elements which is raised to isolate or integrate the area with the rest; and the architectural elevation of its upper level, from whose red dividing wall a simple platform with metal railings projects, which evokes small modernist balconies.

The tenth apartment is distinguished by the peculiar arrangement of the main bedroom and the toilet area: the first is treated as a free-standing box placed in the centre of the main room which can be moved as convenient; the second is an oval semitransparent space made of a combination of perspex and bamboo, articulated on two communicating levels by a short metal stairway with cane steps. In apartment 13 it is the system connecting the levels which surprises spectacularly. This is organised with suspended ladders and walkways and the recurrent application of metal, wood and bamboo. The lightness in the planes and the naturalness of the changes in direction make this interior a brilliant example of the domination of space.

These three examples are emblematic of Rüdiger Lainer and Gertraud Auer's work in the new residential complex in the Viennese Hermanngasse. With a notable reduction in expressive and economic means, the architects managed to create a unitary atmosphere of elegant visual quality in the distinct spaces, only to then individualise them by introducing architectural fragments which order the contents and provide effective aesthetic stimuli in the interior. The design was based on bold ideas such as the dignifying of communal or social

Interior walls are built up into bold blocks of colour to avoid regularity of space.

housing and the need for clients to be involved in the planning process. The final result shows the enormous possibilities of investigation in this wide field of human existence which has frequently been ignored.

Many of the rooms are virtual statements against the rectangle.

The house is replete with unexpected nooks and corners of great character.

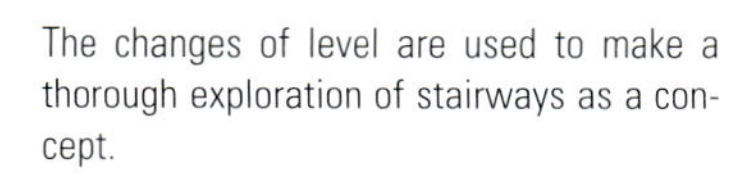

The changes of level are used to make a thorough exploration of stairways as a concept.

The simplicity of line shown in this staircase strikes a harmonious note with the light filtering down from above.

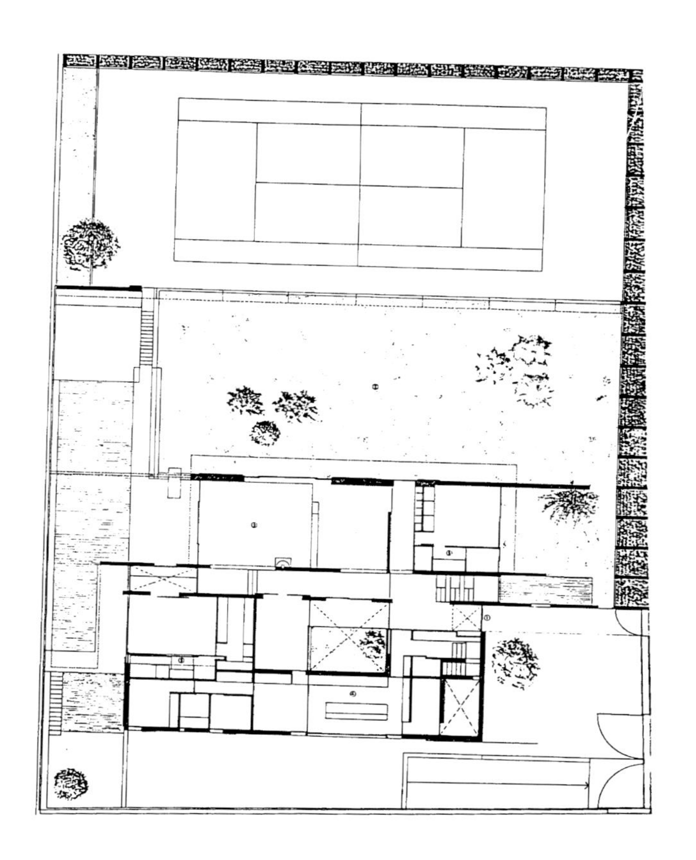

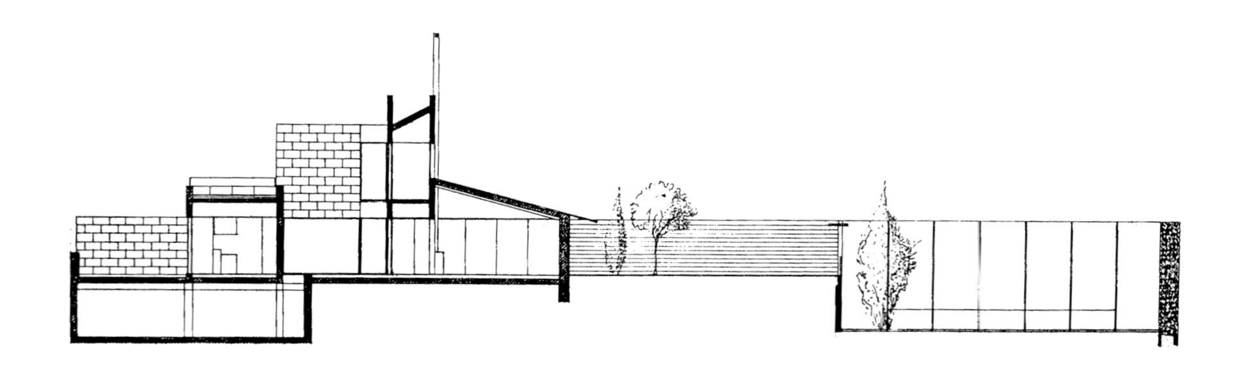

Ground plan of the site.

Cross section of the house and garden.

Casa Nassia

Tonet Sunyer

Tonet Sunyer has devoted much of his career to the construction and remodelling of houses. The project for Nassia House, awarded the FAD prize for interior design in 1989, offered the architect a specific space in which to realize the plastic concepts that govern all of his professional work. Two basic goals guided the architect's original plan: firstly, to adapt the structural form to the topography of the site and secondly, to integrate the interior with the exterior surroundings. The house represents the successful conclusion of a process that combined the spaces, volumes and transparencies to result in this intervention.

The site is located on the slopes of Tibidabo, the lofty hill that overlooks Barcelona on the north. Since the end of the nineteenth century this area has been considered an ideal location for large family residences, offering an escape from the chaos of the city and contact with the countryside and the views. Thus the villa had to be properly positioned in order to obtain the finest perspectives and to become part of the natural environment. With these objectives, the house was slightly oriented towards the west, and Sunyer used the unevenness resulting from the gentle slope of the land to arrange the house and its facilities on the different heights. Two vast east-west terraces levelled the irregularities of the surface.

These two large platforms were adapted to the lie of the land, which eliminated the need for expensive construction techniques. This simple operation established a clear differentiation between the house and

The warm tones of the walls and floors are enhanced by the concealed lighting.

The rich, deep colours and understated lines of the furnishings complement the warmth of the wood.

its immediate context. The eastern orientation offered the maximum amount of free space around the structure, with the outdoor facilities concentrated on the west side and the access to the house on the east elevation. The topography is smoothly adapted to the functional requirements and leisure facilities of the programme.

The tennis court is on the lower platform, and the larger, more versatile one accommodates the house with its rectangular courtyard/garden. On this latter surface the structures and facilities that constitute the nucleus of the project are distributed. A cross section reveals the following sequence from west to east: the tennis court, the garden, the living room with its sloping roof, the partition wall, the interior of the house, and the entrance, with a ramp that leads to the parking area.

This layout can be extended when viewed from the point of view of the ground plan. The overall surface is an irregular rectangle in which only the lower terrace has a perfect shape. The perimeter of the courtyard is definitely rectangular, but it is extended on the north side in a quadrangular section that links the space to the enclosed living room. The swimming pool to the south is also partially regular but, on the side closest to the house, a lounge area is included that modifies its geometrical form. The design of the facilities is subordinate to the volumetric configuration of the house. An examination of the structure from the exterior provides a more thorough understanding of the project.

The entrance facade on the east offers a view of solid, simple superimposed volumes that form the two-storey

villa. The design is cool and linear, with the exception of the parallel walls and the ramp down to the parking area. The west elevation, with the courtyard and swimming pool, has a more dynamic, less rigid form that initiates an interplay with these facilities. Above the courtyard is the inclined stainless steel roof of the living room and above that is the first floor with symmetrically placed windows which draw the setting into the composition. Above the swimming pool the facade is extended toward the south to form a space for relaxation. Although they are situated at the same level, the garden and the swimming pool are almost unrelated, acting as independent entities in order to fulfil the functionally differentiated purposes called for by the programme. A small flight of stairs spans the swimming pool and tennis court levels.

Although the linear sequence is simple and clear, the articulation of the elements is highly complex. The guiding principle underlying this arrangement is the interpenetration of the rooms of the house and the exterior spaces defined in the ground plan. This is achieved specifically throughout the bottom floor. The differentiation between the living room and the rest of the house is very clearly marked. The inclined stainless steel roof acts as a kind of enclosure for the living room, which serves as a transition between the residence and the setting. The living room and the exterior are related by vast picture windows at both ends and along the walls. The space more nearly resembles a gallery than an interior room.

The importance of the glazing goes beyond its communicative function; it also deliberately takes full

Spaciousness and purity of line are the most striking qualities of the kitchen.

Metal is used in carefully distributed elements to provide occasional spots of contrast with the wood and the predominantly warm walls.

Partial view of the dining room. The simple lines of the furniture are very much in keeping with the design as a whole.

The spacious, well-lit living room, with the fireplace on the left.

The upstairs corridor is a fusion of warm colours and cold lines

advantage of the natural light, a crucial element of a Mediterranean climate. The placement of the house on the site was governed by the architect's desire to obtain the best quality of light and the most arresting visual perspectives. The children's bedrooms are on the first floor, where the long corridor with its symmetrically placed windows acts as an organizing principle based on repetition, a means of articulation reminiscent of hotel layouts.

The interior architecture is characterized by similar circulation routes. The living room and the rest of the house are connected by a passageway that runs the length of the ground floor and acts as a partition. This corridor spans the differences in the levels through short flights of steps that are longer at the northern access to the exterior. The roofs are developed through ceilings with a west-east slope that becomes horizontal in the living room.

The interior design belongs to a tradition that seeks stimulation from the aesthetic. The choice of materials used for the furnishings and the finishes is an attempt to express the interpretation of luxury propounded by the second-generation Modernists, such as R.J. Neutra and R. Schindler. Sunyer's aesthetic is radically opposed to the concept of luxury as conceived by the standards of the Victorians and exemplified by the language of Venturi and later theoreticians of Modernism.

Accordingly, the interior design reflects an almost aristocratic simplicity and avoids an ornateness that would endanger the architectural achievements of the

Steps leading up to the ground floor entrance, with the boundary wall on the left.

Plan of the first floor.

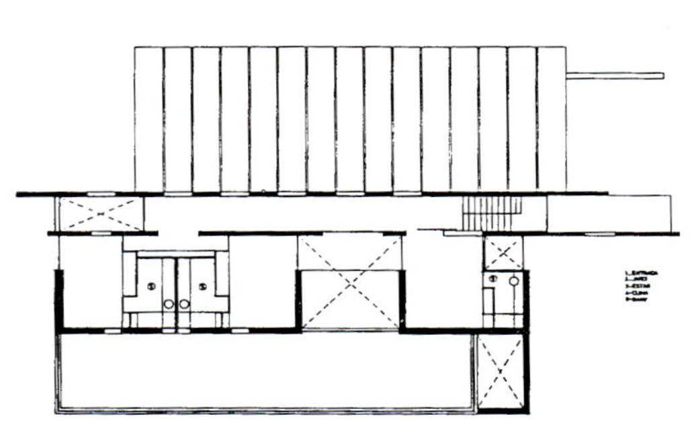

structure. The materials are conventional, but Sunyer has selected the finest: brickwork, metalwork, stainless steel, marble and wood. The flooring of the entire house is done in warm tones of wood, and steel is used in the roofs and free-standing elements. The perimeter of the estate is bounded by structures of great organizational rigour that reveal the architectural treatment given to the outer enclosure.

The exterior appearance is unified by its chromatic treatment. The various materials (wood, brick and marble) are finished in shades of white, with the exception of the walkways to the house from the public roadway or from the car park, whose paving is darker. Through this unifying dimension, the house asserts its identity in the setting.

The interior is distinguished by the linearity of the planes and the transparencies provided by the extensive use of glass. The rooms open onto each other; one can move through the free-flowing space of the house without encountering any visual or physical obstacles. In this way, the impression of interior constriction is avoided, maximum use is made of the available space and fine visual perspectives are obtained from all vantage points.

Through smooth surfaces, a repertoire of high-quality materials and the attractive combination of furniture, this house expresses a concept of elegance based on the language of modern architecture and simplicity of design. All the interior solutions, once they were adapted to the definition of volumes imposed by the topography and were integrated with the external environment, represent a perfect realization of Sunyer's initial intentions.

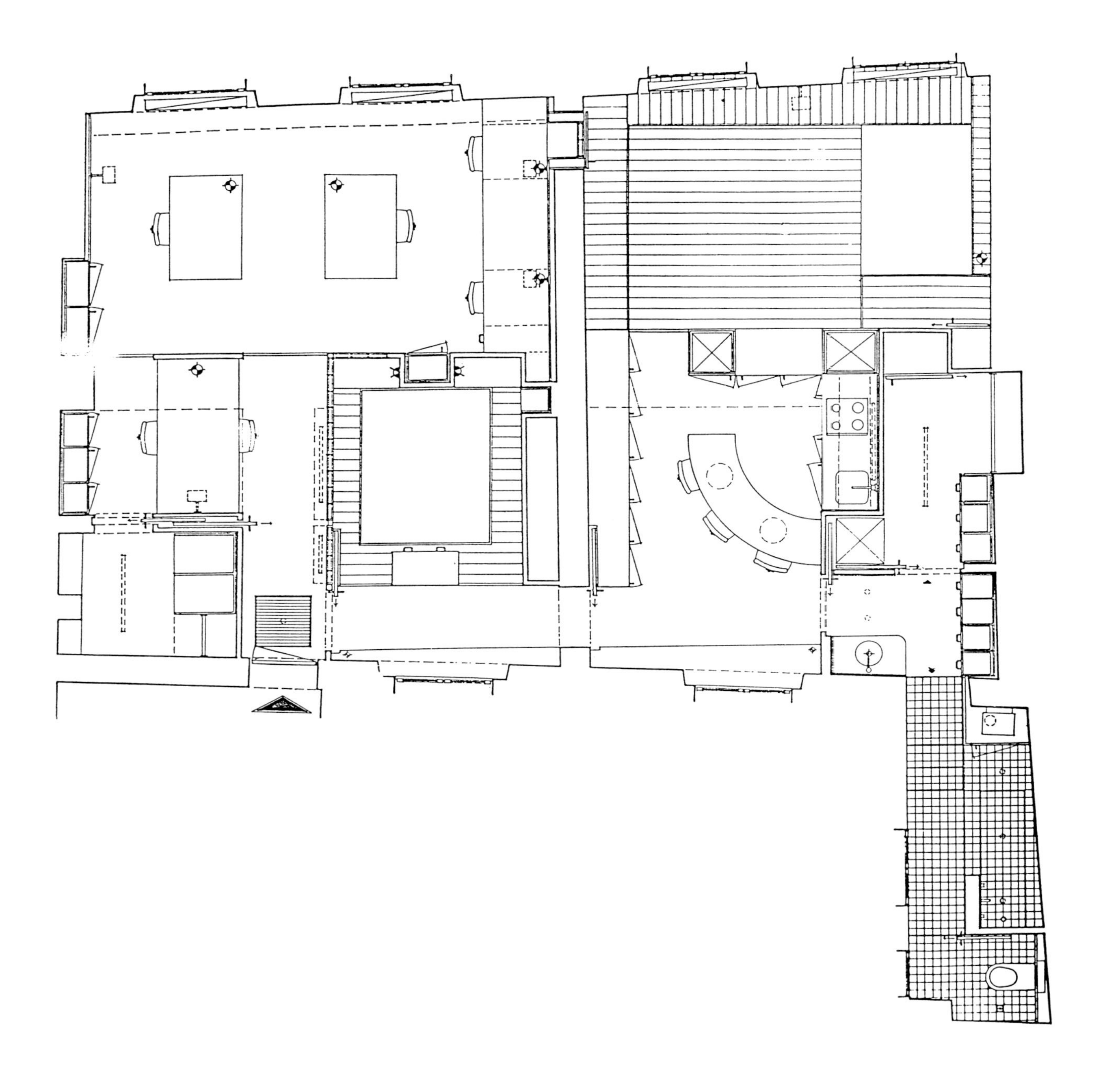

Plan of the studio.

Studio-Appartement

Denis Colomb

This project is a highly explicit illustration of the planning of his own domestic and work spaces. The act of personalizing the interior architecture and decor entails certain risks, such as excess and passion, that frequently interfere with a lucid and methodical development of the residential programme. In-so-far as possible, Colomb has avoided these common mistakes, opting for a design that pursues practicality and comfort within a peaceful, relaxed environment. To accomplish this, he has established firm limits between his office and studio and the areas reserved for private life. Nevertheless, the separation is only physical; there is a uniform, harmonious atmosphere based on a monochromatic treatment, an economy in ornamentation, and overall soft lighting.

Denis Colomb was enthusiastic about the space he selected to live and work in. In 1984 he discovered the apartment, located right in the centre of Paris, and immediately decided that this would be his permanent home. But it was not until 1988 that he was able to begin the major remodelling tasks, which were completed in May of that same year.

The characteristics of this flat, typical of Parisian architecture in the mid nineteenth century, are a rectangular floor plan, with a small trapezoid joined perpendicularly to the right end. The total surface area of the flat is about 110 m^2, with a central bearing wall that divides the space into two almost identical sections. This bipartite structural composition was perfectly suited to the two-fold programme, which would benefit both from

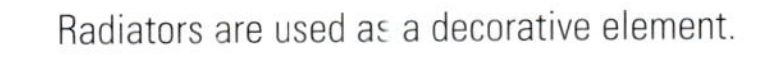

The kitchen is compact yet harmonious and open to the rest of the living space.

Radiators are used as a decorative element.

a vital independence, as well as from a close connection.

From the beginning, practicality was the main planning principle. The presence of the architectural barrier resulted in a division that did not fully meet the requirements of each of the aspects of the programme. As is usually the case, the residential programme required more space than the unpretentious work area, consisting of two essential rooms: a planning studio and an office for receiving clients. The basic differentiation was approached from the standpoint of spatial symmetry; the left side accommodates the work area, while the living space is distributed in the right side.

However, this elementary organization did not fulfil the needs of both aspects of the programme. For this reason a certain amount of space was taken away from the public domain and turned over to domestic activities. Thus, the bedroom was assigned to the left side, representing a break with the symmetry of the plan, but favouring the essential relationship between function and space and the creation of a serene, relaxed atmosphere.

The first of these areas, conceived as an office and a studio, includes the entrance, so that clients can come and go without infringing on the daily activities of the more private sections of the flat. The entrance is distinguished by a sliding door with an opening in stainless melamine, created by the planner himself, by the soft lighting provided by the spotlights set in Cosmo glass brick, and by the neutral cement flooring. Two corridors, positioned at right angles, offer access to the two essential areas. The first corridor communicates with

A view through the hatch and into the kitchen, showing the crescent-shaped bar.

the various work spaces. The sequence of rooms consists of a filing and photocopying area, then the reception office and finally the large studio, the focal point of this section. The first two rooms intercommunicate to facilitate coordination tasks. The furnishing of the reception office is executed in white lamina in order to offer an impression of hospitality.

The corridor leads directly to the studio, which takes up almost half of this section and is designed to make maximum use of the available space. This workroom reveals Colomb's stylistic methodology, based on practicality, on the rejection of superfluous elements and on the definition of a serene, relaxed environment, appropriate for work. The monochromatic use of white throughout the flat contributes to the creation of a neutral

The bedhead is equipped with the same sturdy lamps as are used elsewhere in the apartment.

View into the studio area, showing one of the drawing tables.

The entrance to the bedroom, by means of a sliding door. The carpet provides a rich contrast to the neutral floor covering elsewhere.

setting of great transparency, which is also favoured by the skilful placement of the exterior openings. Both the walls and the various built-in cabinets that reach the ceiling are finished in white print magnetic lamina, providing a vast plain surface to hang plans and sketches. The only elements that interrupt the space are two large drafting tables designed by Colomb, occupying a central position, and a generous work surface with two additional sections. All of these surfaces are 95 cm in height. The chairs, made by Franckel Industries, are high and ergonomic, and their casters facilitate movement, comfort, and maximum operational efficiency. The artificial lighting consists of industrial halogen bracket lights in galvanized steel.

The same fundamental criteria govern the conception of the private sections, but the two aspects of the programme are sharply differentiated. The bedroom is on the left, its area delimited by the angle formed by the two corridors, the studio and the dividing wall. The interior designs of the bedrooms and the workrooms complement each other. For example, the band of glass bricks in the walls common to the corridors and the workroom, and its highly expressive right-angled turn, determines the appearance of those partitions. Thus the wall facing the reception desk is characterized by this unusual horizontal opening, which is countered by the verticality of a stylized structure of metal strips.

The morphology of the studio also affects the structure of the bedroom. One of the built-in cabinets (a technique he uses frequently to make the most of the space, without interrupting its overall neutrality)

An element of spatial variety is introduced into the long, narrow bathroom by the change of floor level that delimits the shower.

penetrates the bedroom area, forming a projection that orders the different components. This small vertical volume is complemented by the two horizontal structures that serve as a night table and a headboard. The bed takes up almost the entire area, resting directly on the floor, which in this room is of unpolished oak to emphasize the warmth of the setting. The most striking design elements are the Jielde hinged lights, which are directed at the frontal wall to create an effective interaction of diffusion and reflection.

The domestic programme is distributed in the right half of the flat, with a sharp differentiation made between the living spaces and the toilet facilities. The former, consisting of the living room and the kitchen/dining room, enjoys a range of windows, and the absence of

Detail of the bathroom, dominated by the simplicity of white ceramic and stainless steel.

Stripped wooden shutters provide a contrast to the light tones and smooth textures.

structural dividers facilitates a uniform diffusion of light. The structural development of the toilet facilities, in contrast, is defined by their function. Most of these spaces are in the small module perpendicular to the main floor plan.

The plan executed by the French architect is contained and relaxing, and, in spite of its two-fold programme, the interior is pervaded by a harmonious atmosphere. The essential features of the flat are its monochrome finish (white, neutral and very light) and the uniformity of the materials employed (stainless steel, grey polished concrete and oak). In this overall basic context of subtlety and efficiency only a few elements stand out: the curved table in the kitchen, the band of glass bricks in the bedroom and the constructed levels. Denis Colomb's project is not consciously minimalist, but it represents the pursuit of the essential, in the pragmatic sense, to create the best possible space for both working and living.

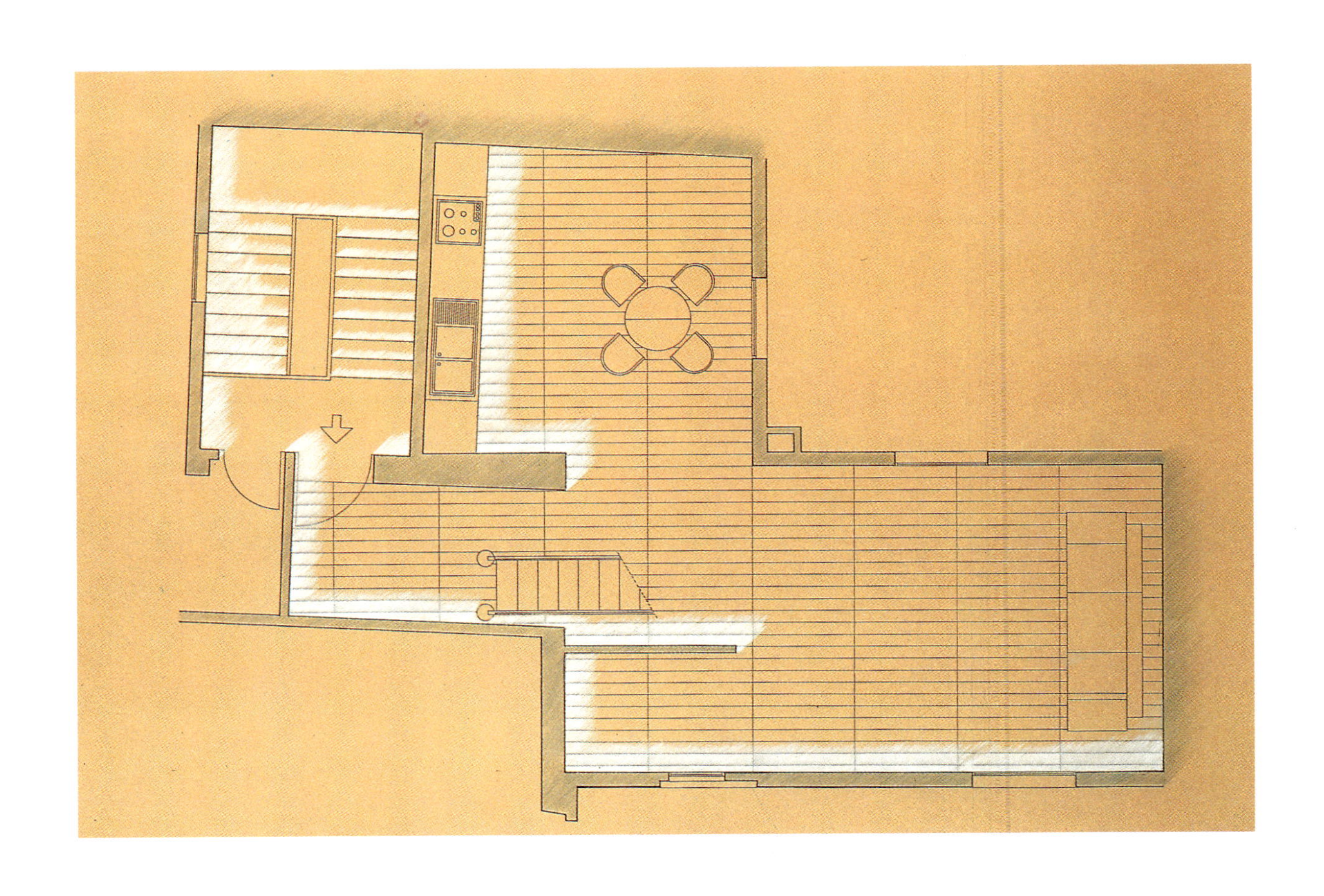

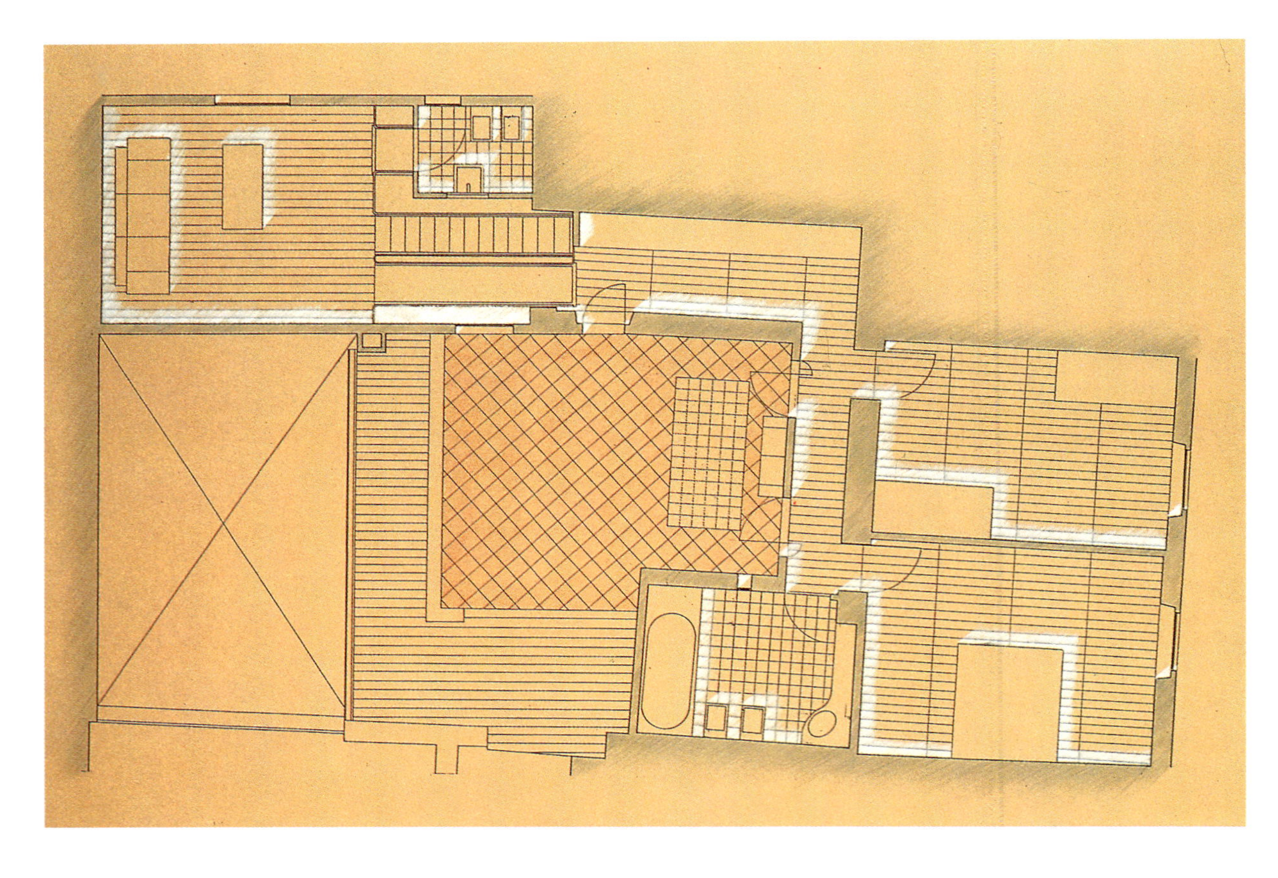

Plan of the lower level.

Plan of the upper level.

Appartamento in Via dell'Oriolo

Fabrizio Fabietti & Achille Michelizzi

Situated in the historic centre of the city of Florence, this recent work by the Achille Michelizzi and Fabrizio Fabietti team involves a series of recurring thematic ideas in the field of residential interior design: the most efficient use of available space, the maintenance of unbroken perspectives, attention to the communication systems between floors, and the combination of innovative components and materials with those that are clearly traditional.

In the specific case of this apartment, the authors had to intervene in two adjoining buildings to design a unified volume. The most obvious risks in such a unification process is the creation of two different milieus, which would not be suitable for the type of residential interior design they are attempting to express. To make the most of the internal space of these adjacent flats, a floor slab was introduced to create two levels, thus facilitating the room distribution. The danger of losing the impression of unity was avoided through the creation of a double-height space to accommodate the different circulation systems. One of the most important innovations of the project is the suspended, independent and transparent arrangement of these connecting structures.

The site of this project is in the historic quarter of Florence, about 100 m from the Santa Maria dei Fiori Cathedral. The point of departure for the plan might have been the expression of the classical spirit of this historic district. However, a traditional treatment would have made the solution of several characteristics of this rather indifferent volume very difficult.

The bridge at the top of the stairwell. Windows and doors are in a playful variety of shapes.

The renovation of the apartment was based on several criteria that included the recovery of the upper areas and the creation of exterior complementary spaces, which neither of the existing buildings enjoyed. The volume benefited from a heightened vertical tendency, which enabled the introduction of a second level for the development of an important part of the programme. A sector of the roof was converted into a terrace to establish a link between the interior of the residence and its extraordinary setting in the Italian city.

After the division of the spaces, which also served to unify them, the next conflict arose from the interior diversification of the various planes and heights, which would be detrimental to the domestic programme. In addition to the differentiation of atmospheres, the introduction of structural obstacles also involved the risk of losing the interior visual perspectives and directional tendencies of the whole. The architects had to solve this problem without sacrificing any usable space or any of the pragmatic aspects of the programme.

With this in mind, they turned to a technique that is frequently used in contemporary domestic interiors: an opening in the floor slab. There are two common procedures. A platform over one sector is introduced, leaving a double-height space (both physical and visual) for one of the more important rooms, usually the living room or the dining room. The other technique makes use of a floor slab over the entire surface with an opening in it to organize the vertical and horizontal tendencies along this core axis. Michelizzi and Fabietti chose the second

View from under the stairs into the kitchen-dining room, where antique furniture stands alongside fitted stainless steel cupboards.

The sweeping lines of the stairway lead the eye up towards the upper floor.

The dynamic stairway and bridge afford views of both levels and a glimpse into the patio.

The arched interior doors contrast with those leading on to the patio.

View out across the dining table showing the eclectic mixture of decorating styles.

option because of the particular difficulties of the spatial qualities of the volume; although their two areas had been joined, differences still existed in the two layouts.

The basic arrangement of the functional programme is ordered by the levels. On the ground floor the entryway opens onto a small reception area with a stairway leading to the upper level. The articulating space is visible from this area. Around that space are the kitchen/dining room and a generous living room with a communicating library. There is a bathroom above the library that bounds the central atrium on the upper level. Also on that level are the bedrooms, distributed by connecting hallways that maintain the interior perspective. The exterior terrace is of major significance to the design. Its grand entrance provides both floors with natural light by means of the central opening.

Achille Michelizzi's and Fabrizio Fabietti's main achievements in this apartment on the Florentine Via dell'Oriolo are based on new approaches to techniques that are frequently employed by interior designers. The strategies of the second level and the opening in the floor slab were developed through masterly procedures that achieve an even diffusion of natural light, while preserving the maximum interior perspectives. Thus, unique modes of perception exist between the two floors of the residence, created by the glazed walkway and the suspended bridge. A harmonious atmosphere results from the functional differentiation of the service and living areas, with a treatment that ranges from the most stately and classical to the most modern and innovative.

Drawing of the east elevation.

Drawing of the house and lap pool.

Drawing of the west elevation.

New interpretation of a regional style

Ross S. Anderson of Anderson & Schwarz Architects

This small 1500-square-foot house, overlooking Napa Valley, California, is a guest cottage and pool house for a future main residence. It is situated on a slightly sloping site at the top of a hill, and enjoys extensive views of the whole valley. Seen from the foot of the hill, the house stands out against the green vegetation and the blue sky almost like a fairy-tale castle.

The house combines humble materials and a regional imagery in a simple, country structure that maintains tension in its composition and playfulness in its form. The house itself was completed in 1987 and the swimming pool in 1989.

The architect was Ross S. Anderson, of Anderson & Schwarz. Anderson graduated from Stanford University in 1973 and took his master's in Architecture at the Harvard Graduate School of Design. After gaining experience in various architectural firms he set up his own practice in 1981. He has lectured at several universities such as Yale University and Virginia Polytechnic Institute and has also participated in major exhibitions both in the USA and Europe. These include "Architectural Art" at the American Crafts Museum, New York; the Venice Biennial in Venice, Italy; and "Architects for Social Responsibility" at the Protech Gallery, New York. During his long career, his work has been awarded many important prizes, including an Honourable Mention in the Oberlin Bandstand competition; 40 Under 40, Interiors *magazine; and Record Houses, Architectural Record, for this house in the Napa Valley.*

Floor plan of the lower level.

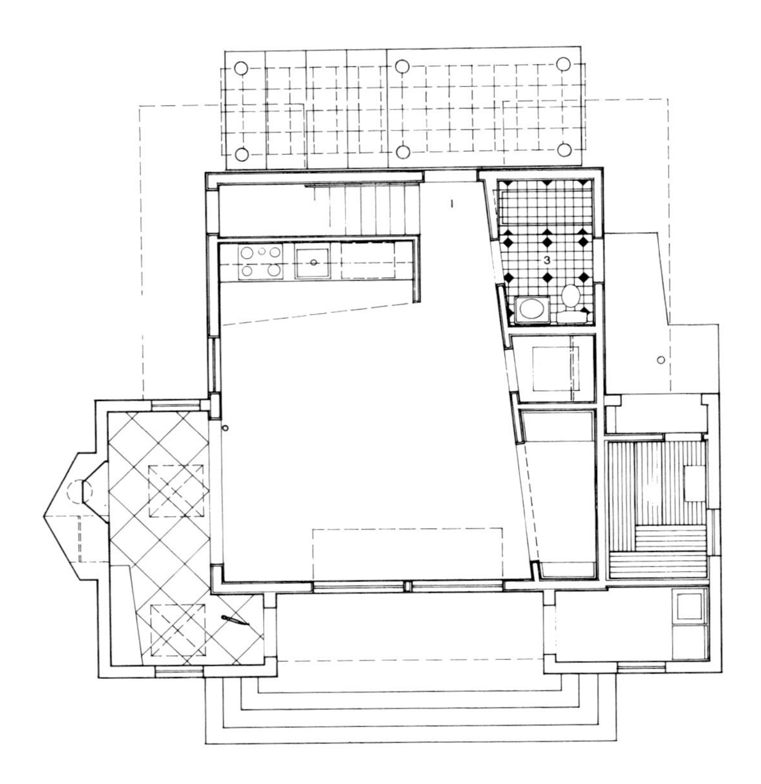

Floor plan of the upper level, which houses the bedrooms.

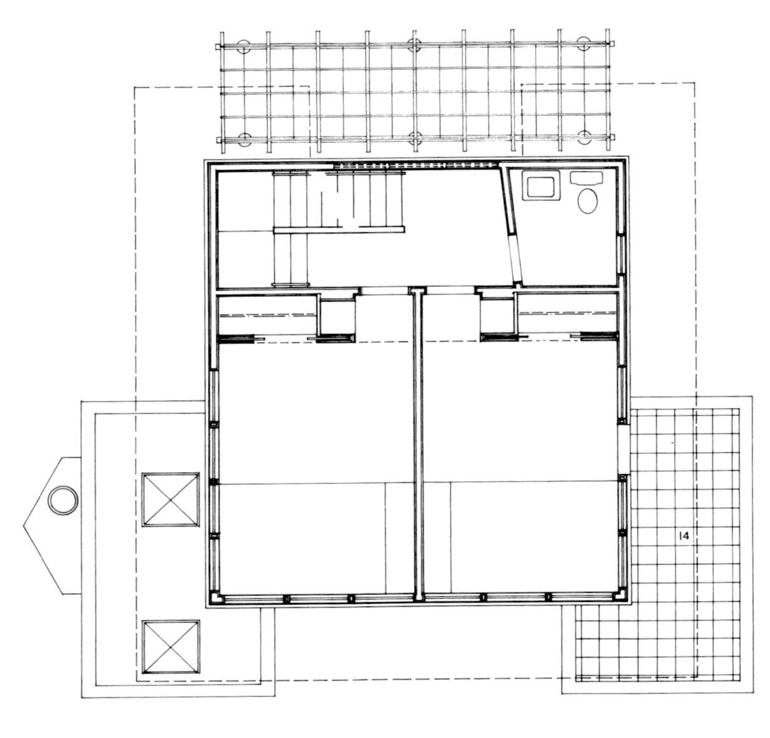

The thick lower walls of the cottage are framed in 2 x 6's and the upper in 2 x 4's. All the inside perimeter walls are sheathed with a transparent-stained plywood, maintaining the integrity of the wooden box throughout the house. Much like an old box camera, this house captures the view of the valley below and allows it to be savoured time and time again.

The interior elements extend the volume of the house out through the large, south-facing window and down, past the pool, directing one's view toward the valley and vineyards below. The main entrance leads directly into the living/dining room which corresponds to the large window on the south side of the exterior wall. Two sofas, one against the wall and the other in front of a glass table, complete the furnishings. The fireplace is set into one of the concrete blocks. The kitchen is next to the living room, all in wood and with chairs painted pale green. This floor also houses a storeroom, sauna and outdoor shower.

Responding to the insistent squeezing of the two concrete brackets, the second floor telescopes up from within the redwood-sheathed box below. The bedrooms with en suite *bathroom are on this floor. These rooms are well lit through the strip windows on the south wall. The interior decor is simple and austere, and all the rooms have access to an exterior terrace with views of the valley below.*

On the upper, attic level, the house gathers itself under the exposed framing of the roof and dormers. This large room at the top of the stairs is used as a bedroom.

Plan of the attic.

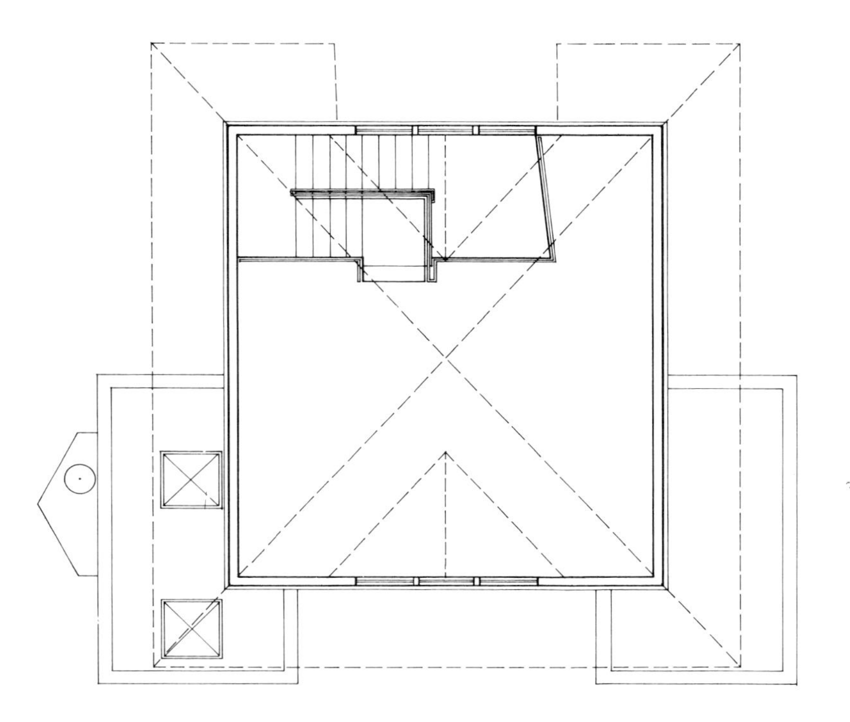

0 1 5 10

Drawing of south elevation.

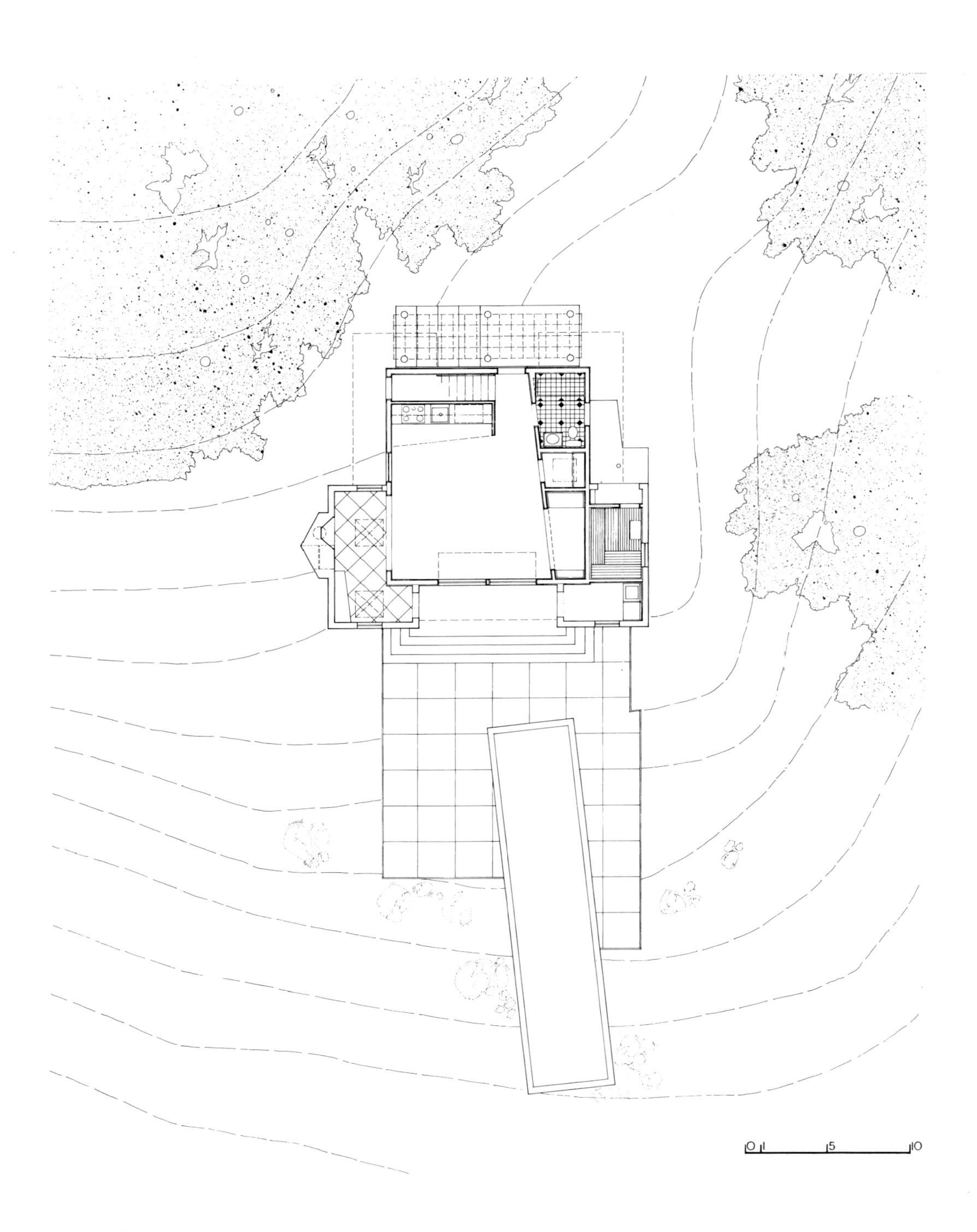

General plan of the construction and its surroundings.

Close-up of the south facade showing the magnificent lap pool.

The attic houses this bedroom under the triangle roof.

The sitting room commands a magnificent view over the pool and the valley below.

Close-up of one of the built-in wooden beds.

A futon-style bed, a scattering of soft cushions, two bedside tables and a chair are the only furnishings in the room. The triangular window and crossed beams of the roof complete the decor. The view from the attic is of the pines and oaks of the upper part of the valley behind the house.

This house in Rutherford, in California's Napa Valley, designed by Ross S. Anderson, is a small building on a mountain top, made of wood and contained and held by two concrete block brackets. It consists of two floors with an attic sheltered beneath a triangular roof. But the most outstanding features of this building are its facades – the northern side, compact and neat, with a pergola housing the main entrance, and the southern side, with panoramic views of the swimming pool and valley through its large windows. The interior of the house is light, simple and cosy. Because of these factors, the house offers its occupants an irresistible invitation to relax and to enjoy the beauty, harmony and sunshine of this privileged setting in the Napa Valley.

Floor plans of each level.

Casa Miramar

Nuri Jolis & Josep Juvé

The rehabilitation of an old building and its adaptation to modern domestic requirements is not a mere exercise in the reinterpretation of volumes and spaces and the modification of structures. Such a project also allows the architect to develop sensitive dialogues between the concepts of the old order and the new; light and darkness; presence and absence. Casa Miramar, the property and work of the young Catalan architects Nuri Jolis and Josep Juvé, is a clear illustration of the successful conditioning of an old building to a contemporary lifestyle, with no loss of its historical essence or of any of the architectural values of this particular local tradition.

The architects were confronted by a three-hundred-year-old building with a main floor and two upper storeys, located in the old quarter of Sitges, a tourist resort on the coast of Catalonia. The successive enlargements and modifications of the house undertaken by former owners had always been in harmony with the principles of the vernacular architecture and the traditional building methods. Thus the building had no contemporary formal or material elements. The original walls were characterized by their considerable thickness and clay fabric with windows placed according to the need for light and ventilation in the interior.

The initial objective of the intervention was to carry out the complete rehabilitation called for by the poor state of preservation of the built structures. From the standpoint of composition, the planners regarded the distribution methods of the vernacular architecture as

Rustic warmth in the furnishings and the unfaced brick arch is played off against the sophistication of the mosaic work.

The swinging glass partition is an element of both integration and separation.

Robust wooden furniture and rich, natural colours harmonise with the structure of the house.

View into the bathroom, showing the foot of the stone staircase.

Rough lines, textures and angles give the house its character.

highly satisfactory qualitative values. But the serious deterioration of the residence demanded, as a first stage, the reinforcement and restructuring of the entire frame, in order to transform the house into a livable space with a sufficient guarantee of physical safety and, most important of all, to retain its traditional essence within the typological context.

The planning process for the exterior was chiefly focused on the latter goal: to avoid disrupting its integration and formal role in the fabric of the old quarter of the city. For that reason, the task was essentially one of restoration, preserving all the elements that were still in good condition and replacing the deteriorated structures with new ones, using building materials similar to the original (as is the case of the wooden pergola of the second-storey balcony). Thus, white stucco coexists with the original stone in continuous sections or with areas left bare, offering evidence of the historical past of the building.

In contrast, the task of restructuring the interior was planned with an eye to the functional requirements of a second home, but making sure that the programme would allow its use as a permanent residence. The building was conceived as a living space for three people, with a small studio and office that suggest the eventual return of the need to combine residential and professional premises. The small dimensions of all three floors of the house (each about 40 m^2) provided the motivation underlying the basic objective of creating multipurpose rooms that would be as open as possible, *in order not to interrupt the internal dynamic with divisions or needless limits. On the basis of this set of pertinent conditions, most of the work was planned on the site rather than in the studio.*

The first stage involved demolishing all the structural components that were either in poor condition or inappropriate for the new programme, in order to uncover the essential frame of the building. Partition walls and closets added in earlier renovations were destroyed until the bare skeleton was revealed, and the elementary qualities of the original architecture were recovered: a masonry segmental arch, the vault of the stairway, the wooden beams of the floor slabs, the ceramic fragments of the balcony flooring and the single-pitch roof.

In this project, the process of correcting the structural deficiencies made a decisive contribution to the formal result, since resolving the structural conflicts suggested new techniques and approaches. For example, the wooden beams of the ground-floor ceiling were severely deteriorated, so it was decided to reduce their span with the placement of a transverse beam. Through this strategy a triangular false ceiling was created that covers the kitchen area.

The layout was organized on three floors with rather small dimensions. To establish the physical communication between them, a stairway had been built against one of the bearing walls, protected by partitions that closed it off at the respective levels. The architects

At the top of the house, the simple bedroom is bathed in light from the terrace.

Bare rafters and beams are exploited as a decorative feature throughout the house.

The Mediterranean character of the house comes into its own in the ground floor entrance hall.

Alcoves built into the structure of the thick walls are used for shelf space.

The bathroom is a modern interpretation of rustic simplicity.

The irregularity of the flcor plan provides additional interest.

chose to eliminate these formal restrictions, which prevented the diffusion of natural light, particularly on the first floor. This approach gained space and a vertical perspective that integrated the entire house volumetrically and further revealed the architectural and organizational values of the old building.

As we have mentioned, the removal of the safety partitions from the stairway had the most notable effect on the quality of the first-floor environment. Here, cross-ventilation was obtained, as well as the entrance of light from the openings in the main facade and one of the sides of the building. The decision to create two differentiated functional spaces on this floor might have resulted in a serious conflict with these structural achievements. The most effective solution had to be movable and transparent, and for this they introduced a large, glazed window that could be raised all the way up in summer to form a plane parallel to the ceiling. In this way, maximum spatial depth was achieved with an optimal provision for the entrance of light and fresh air.

Once the interior was free of physical obstacles, the distribution was guided by the attempt to create flexible, open spaces, which could freely fulfil diverse functions. The ground floor accommodates the kitchen/dining room area and the living room, conveniently close together for comfort during the cold winter, while the first floor contains a studio, a bedroom and a bathroom. Finally, the top floor is an open area that, depending on the needs of the moment, may serve as a summer living room or a bedroom, with a small adjoining bath and a balcony overlooking the street.

The two main rooms on the first floor can be separated by the swinging partition and a heavy curtain.

On the terrace, the awning provides shade and privacy without excluding light.

Each of these floors has been planned to meet functional demands and reflects the attempt to create a setting, on the basis of visual quality and light, that responds to weather conditions and the season of the year, a major factor in the programme of a second home. On the ground floor, the distinction between the different areas is subtly marked by various components of the architecture, the design and the decor, which replace the usual partition-wall system, the latter not being highly recommended for such a small space. The segmental arch, the slight difference in level between the entrance hall and the rest of the residence, an unconventionally placed hanging, and various pieces of plain, attractive furniture, organize movement in a linear sequence, doing away with the need for a continuous division.

In this project Nuri Jolis and Josep Juvé have elevated the concept of the holiday home without resorting to the exaggerated effects of modern design or to ostentatious luxury. This work suggests the potential for the integration of indigenous architectural values and a contemporary living environment through a process of interior restructuring and decor that reflects the creative sensitivity of these two young Catalan architects.

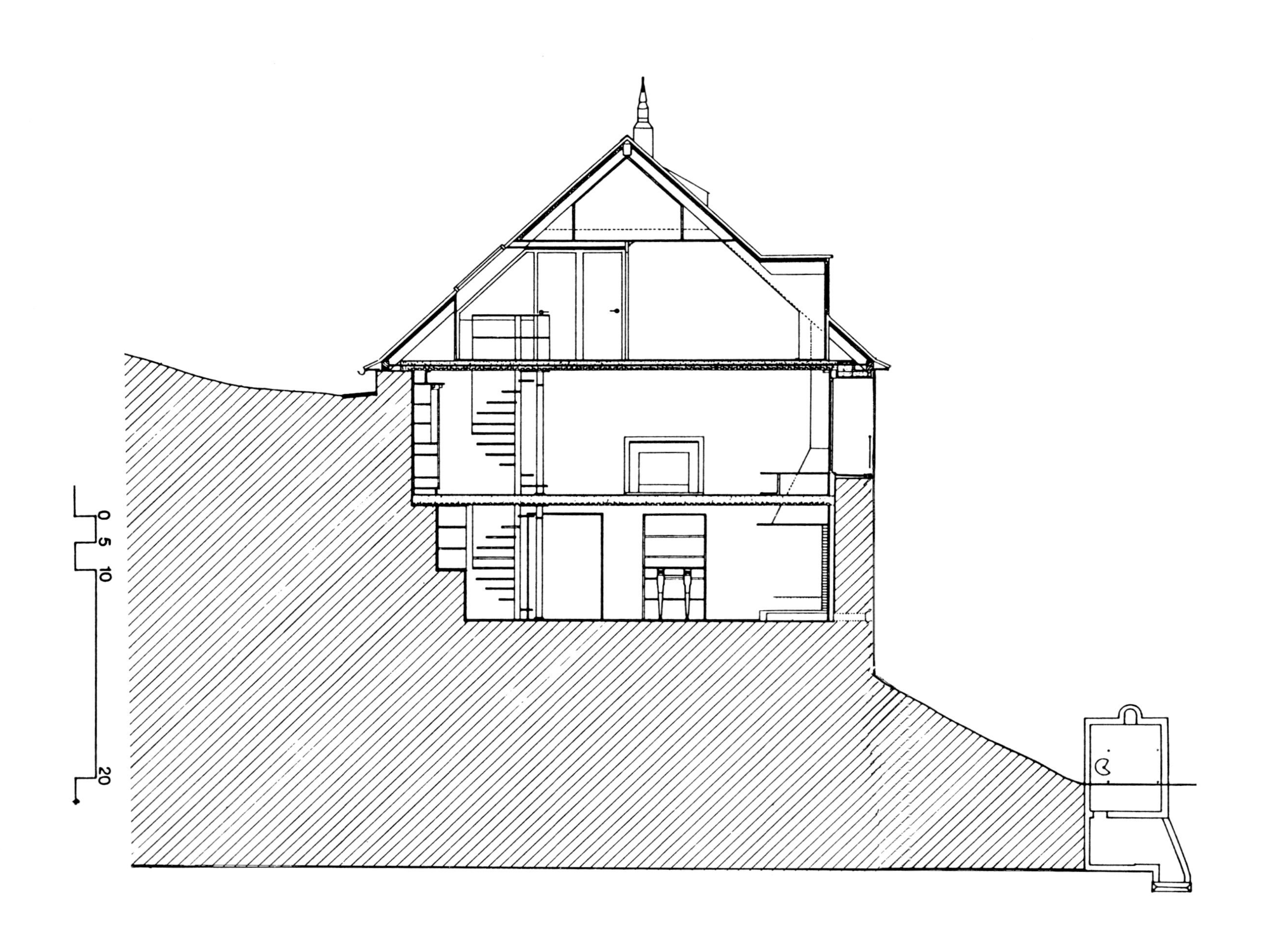
0
5
10
20

Lateral cross section of the house.

Borda d'en Roy

Christian Cirici

Christian Cirici's conversion of Pastor House entailed more than the design of an interior reflecting the formal freedom that distinguishes his work. He had to adapt and condition an existing building without diverging from the values of its vernacular tradition. The project involved preserving the architectural structures that are typical of the setting, and at the same time modernizing the building inside and out to create a comfortable residence whose elegance stems from its simplicity.

The house is located in the town centre of Arrós, in the lower Vall d'Aran in the Catalan province of Lleida. Cirici presented his proposal in 1988 and the construction took the following two years. The building was to be a second home, which called for an innovative treatment of the interior. Before its renovation, the separate two-storey structure was a farm building with an upper level that had been used to store hay and a lower level that had served as a cow barn in the winter. The change in the functional programme was the point of departure for the project.

From the exterior, the original structure was a very simple volume with a hipped roof. It included a south-facing courtyard that provided access to the interior. This was preserved to reinforce the building's continuity with the setting.

The topography of the site presented several drawbacks which, nevertheless, are elements in harmonising the house with the surroundings. The terrain has a steep southern slope where the courtyard is located. Thus the building has a double perspective,

Frontal view of the house, which is perfectly integrated into the Pyrenean landscape.

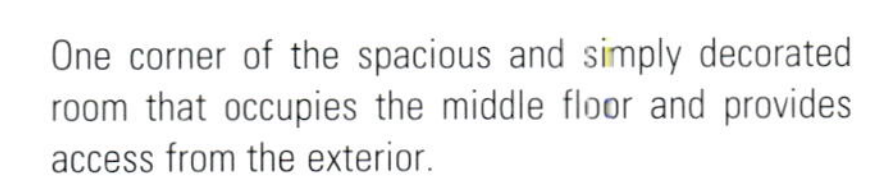

One corner of the spacious and simply decorated room that occupies the middle floor and provides access from the exterior.

viewed from the north or the south. From the north, the house appears as a massive roof over a single storey. From the opposite direction, it has two levels that rise from a retaining wall and natural rock of more than 2 m in height. The enclosure walls are built of dry stone, while the original structure of the roof and the slab that separated the hay loft from the cow barn were built of wood.

Viewing the house from both sides, one can appreciate the way in which the slope of the terrain provides the outside image of the house with an ambiguous dimension. On one side, the house is integrated with the architectural environment as a simple geometrical volume distinguished by a splendid slate hipped roof, typical of the vernacular tradition of the area. From the other side, the exterior offers a better reflection of its true dimensions and all of the aspects of the interior.

The architectural setting called for the maintenance of the exterior characteristics. But this preservation imposed a series of design constraints on the restoration. The basic objective that guided the process was to preserve as far as possible all of the elements that were in good condition and that formed part of the shell. In this way the constant dialogue between the building and the countryside and its tradition would be ensured, and the conversion process would consist, for the most part, of the structural adaptation to the new interior functions.

The reconditioning process was limited to insulating and weather-proofing the interior surfaces of the dry stone walls. The architect wished to avoid the introduction of new elements, accepting only those that

View across the middle floor. Light, modern furnishings predominate, despite the old fireplace.

were indispensable and giving them a treatment similar to the existing components. The most obvious example of this approach is the sloping roof that protects the access to the second floor, in its perfect integration with the rest of the roof. Cirici had no doubt that new openings were required for a country house programme that could not be deprived of the benefits of natural light. The windows received a more inventive treatment: aluminium sheets in lively colours with steel frames painted the same shades. This addition represents an attempt to maintain the tenuous balance between the vernacular and the modern, sophisticated elements which call attention to the contemporary nature of the restoration.

The original structural organization was articulated on two floors. However, the new programme called for the addition of a third level to obtain a better functional arrangement of the rooms. The former entrance through the south-facing courtyard is still the only means of access to the house. There are two entries to the interior: the first is the old door of the cow barn, which opens onto the ground floor; the second includes a flight of steps that leads to the first floor, where the hay used to be stored. This area of the courtyard is partly covered by the slate roof to protect the entrance. The third level, which is newly built, completes the spatial distribution.

The three surfaces are all regular rectangles. The ground floor contains the kitchen/dining room, a rustic fireplace and a guest room and bathroom. The living room takes up the entire surface of the first floor with no physical obstacles to limit the spatial perspective of its

Plan of the middle floor.

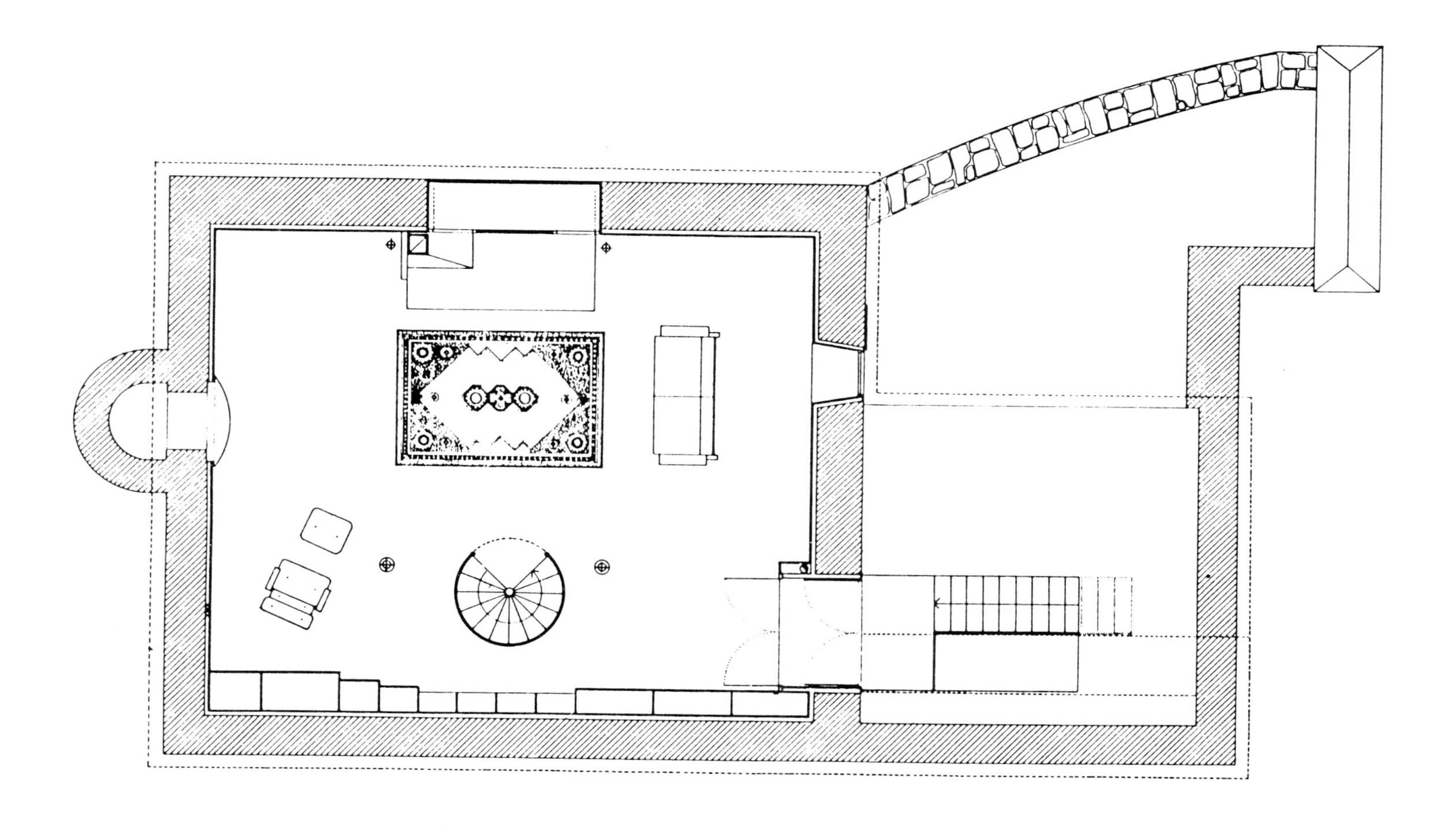

Plan of the lower floor.

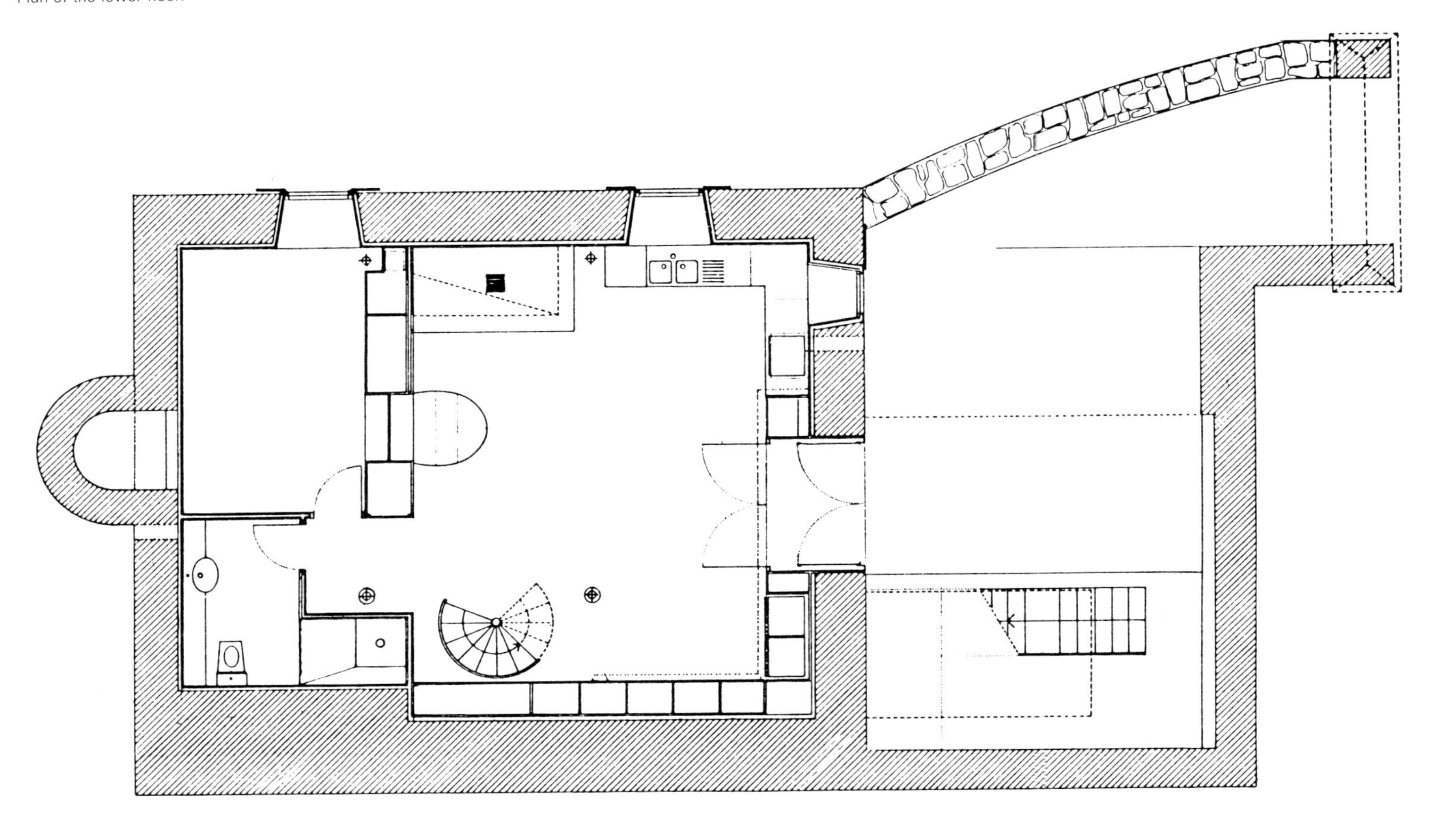

dimensions. The simple, unadorned furnishings and a large picture window increase the impression of spaciousness offered by this room. At the height of the struts of the roof structure, another floor slab is inserted for the bedrooms, whose ceiling is formed by the slopes of the roof. As the top floor of the house, this completes the room distribution.

The materials used reflect the simplicity of the architectural treatment. The exposed pillars and beams are of laminated steel. The pillars are circular while the beams form H sections. The floor slabs are of reinforced concrete and were built on white-enamelled corrugated steel frameworks that were left exposed.

The flooring of the house is of slate on the ground floor and wood on the other two. Marble is used in the bathrooms. In the interior, all of the walls and the ceiling of the top floor are panelled in wood. In the kitchen the panelling is lined with Formica. The rest of the house is surfaced with trowelled stucco.

The appearance of the rooms is defined to a certain extent by the materials used as finishes. On the ground floor the slate and the Formica initiate a highly effective chromatic dialogue between the functional and the rustic that is reinforced by the strategic placement of the windows. The fireplace in exposed brick alludes to the rural setting of the house.

The first-floor living room is the largest space in the house. The sparse furnishing (one sofa, two rocking chairs, a desk and several cabinets and book cases) and the vast picture window facing south all contribute to the

The large window in the centre of the frontage looks out over the valley.

The foot of the staircase, in the stone-paved kitchen downstairs.

sense of spaciousness, lightness and transparency that characterizes the room. The chairs and free-standing elements are arranged around a large carpet whose colours gracefully offset the texture of the wooden flooring. The desk faces the large window that provides the light required for working. The cabinets, bookcases, and other elements built into the architecture are panelled in beechwood, combining well with the flooring and the facing of the walls.

There are bedrooms and two bathrooms on the top floor, which implies a greater organizational separation. The slope of the roof, which is the ceiling of this storey, fosters an interplay of lines and angles that dominates its interior. The skylights on the sloping roof provide a delicate, diffused light. The marble finish of the bathrooms and the stylized fittings complete the design of the second floor.

Finally, there is one structural element that is the most significant of the project. A communication system for the three floors based on flights of stairs would have taken up too much space, restricting the distribution of the programme. The most appropriate solution was a spiral staircase to connect the three levels, allowing maximum advantage to be taken of the available space. However, this link is not only physical; it also succeeds in relating the entire house conceptually, as the stairway becomes the symbol of the new intervention. Its elegant, stylized design is constructed on a steel framework with

The top of the spiral staircase, with the main bathroom beyond.

The lower floor houses the kitchen, e-quipped with an open fireplace.

The flue from the hearth on the floor below rises to one side of the panoramic window.

steps finished in wood. The metal tubes that encircle the openings on each floor have slight kinks, a gesture towards innovation and the avant-garde.

The renovation of Pastor House offered the architect an opportunity to initiate a dialectical exchange between the vernacular architectural tradition and the contemporary aesthetic that contributes to the new functional programme of the house. The slope of the roof, the respect for indigenous materials and the preservation of the dry stone walls express the primary intention. The new openings and the simple, stylized treatment of the interior reflect the new conception. Christian Cirici has succeeded in establishing a complex balance in an elegant, natural manner.

The whole house is articulated around the one-piece spiral staircase.

Plan of the upper floor.

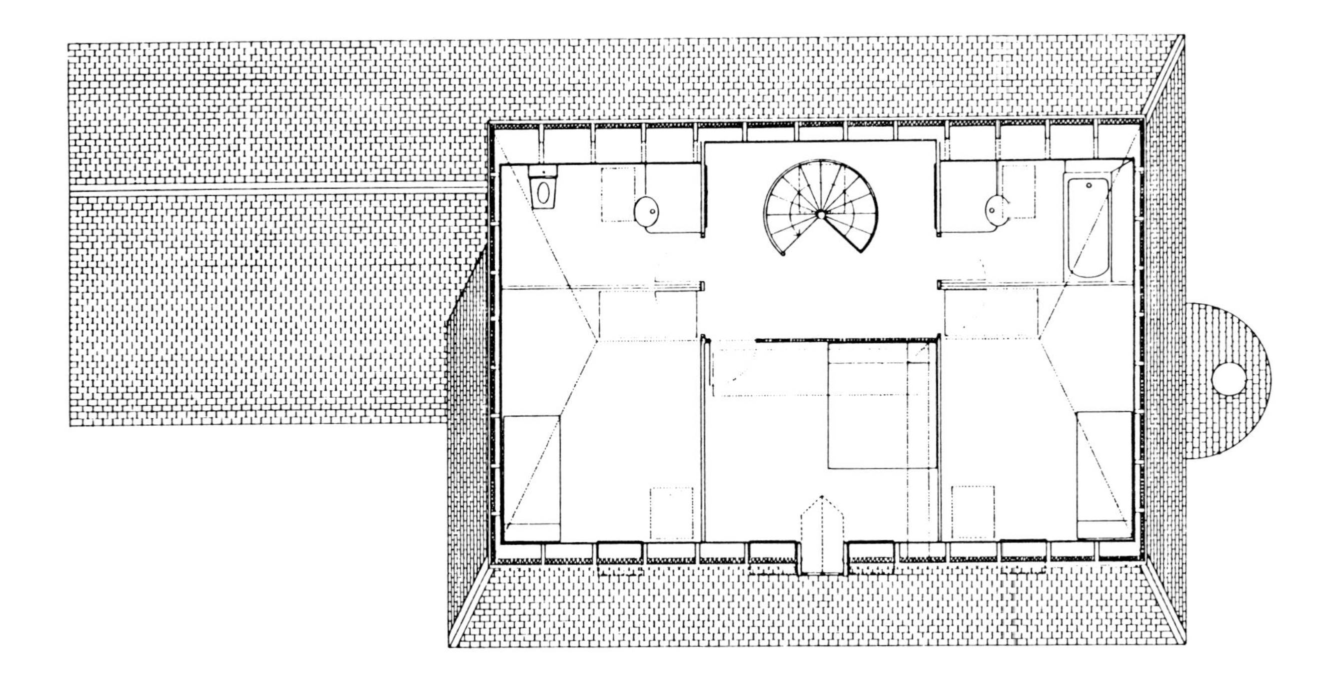

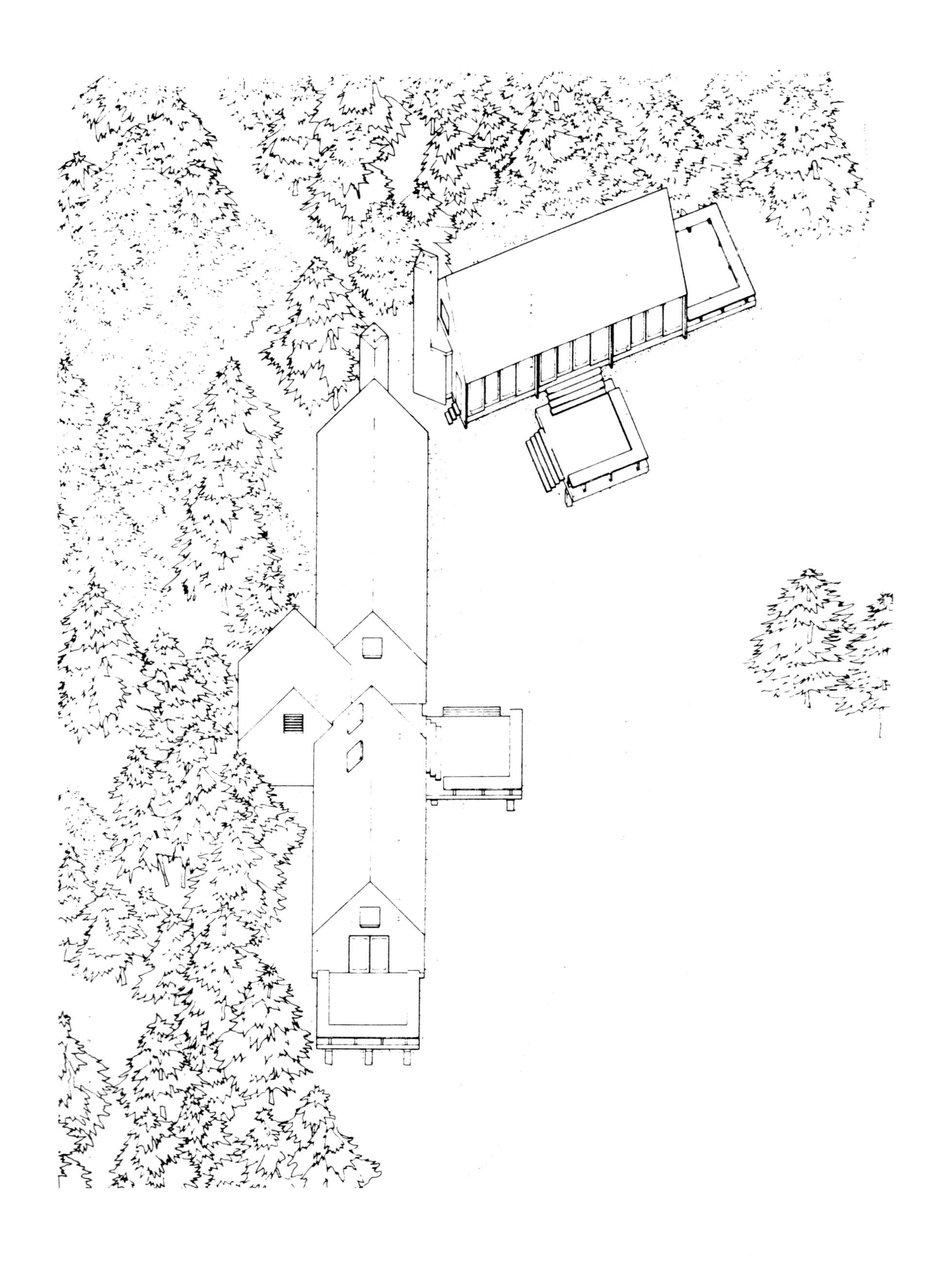

Sketch of the house and surroundings.

Wooden house on pillars

Peter Forbes

This beautiful setting, a fusion of sea, open meadow and wild coniferous forest, provided an excellent starting point for the ideas of Peter Forbes, the architect who built this house. The building is raised on pillars and has large expanses of glass, typical of seaside houses, combined with a wooden construction more common in houses in the mountains, but in this case very appropriate to the surrounding vegetation.

This single-family dwelling is located on Great Cranberry Island, Maine, the easternmost state of the USA. The town is in New England, bathed by the waters of the Atlantic on the Canadian border. This coastal site is at the juncture of a dense, coniferous forest and open meadow and the house articulates and reinforces the natural division of the landscape. The slightly sloping site has a rough, irregular surface. Its privileged situation at the top of a hill affords the occupants a glorious view of almost the entire surrounding area including the marine horizon and a few small islands in the distance.

Peter Forbes studied Architecture at the University of Michigan, graduating in 1966. The following year, he entered Yale University where he received a Master of Architecture. In 1991, he received the title of Doctor of Engineering Technology from the Wentworth Institution of Technology. In 1980 he founded his own firm, Peter Forbes and Associates, Inc., of which he is also president. His academic experience includes a period as visiting professor at the universities of Harvard and Michigan and the Catholic University in Rome. He has also been guest critic at the Technical University of Nova Scotia, Virginia

Elevations of the house.

Plan view of the building.

All of the interior surfaces are covered with a variety of woods, from cedar to mahogany and fir.

All of the furniture is wood, even in the kitchen.

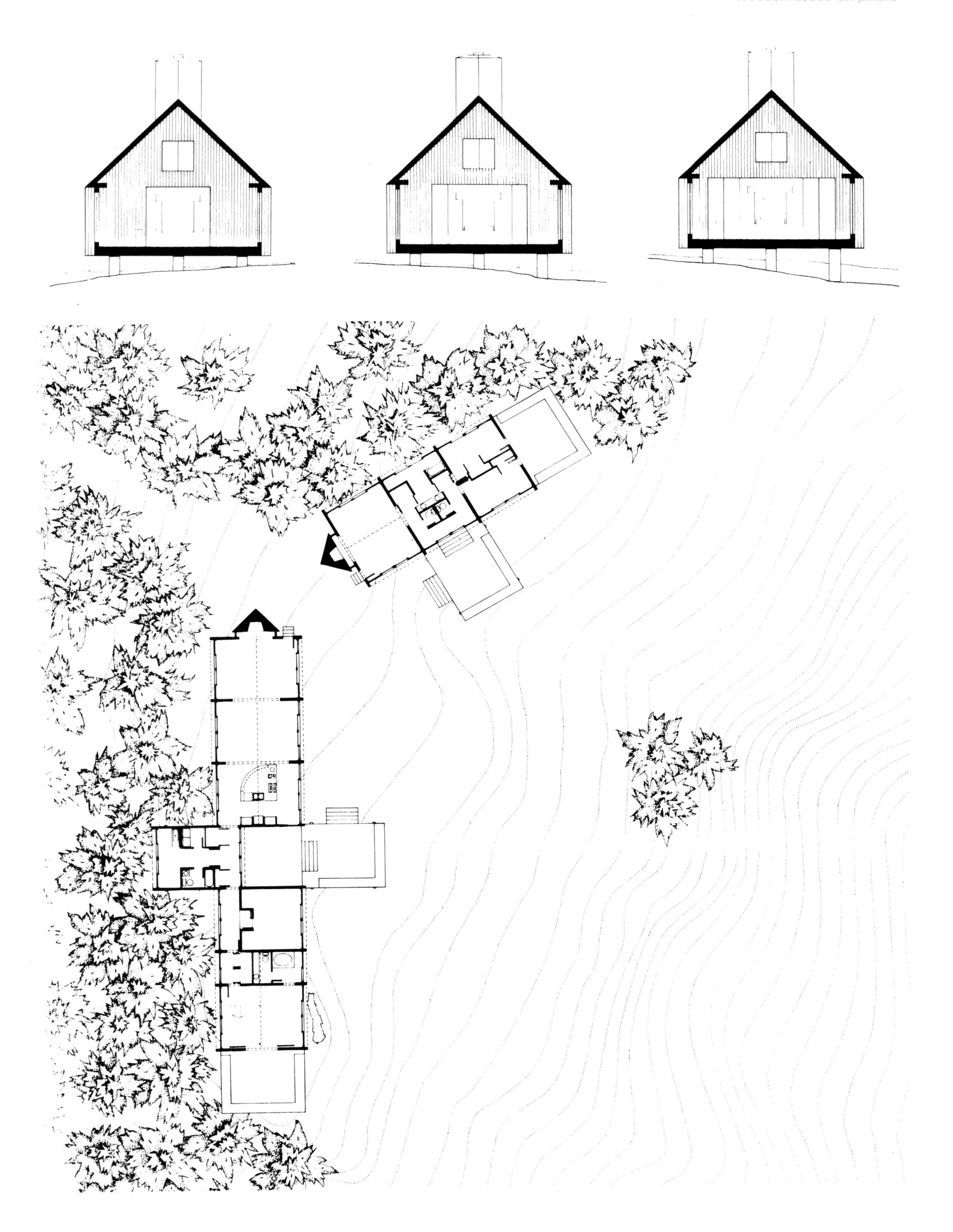

The hearth is of stone, echoing the enormous chimneys outside.

Polytechnic Institute, Boston Architectural Center, Wentworth Institution of Technology, and the Massachusetts Institute of Technology. He was president of the Boston Society of Architects (1989) and the Massachusetts Council of the AIA (1984), and is a member of the American Institute of Architects and National Judicial Council (1986-89). Many of his projects have been published in specialised magazines all over the world, such as Architecture, Architectural Record, A+U, Baumeister, Builder, Metropolitan Home, House Beautiful, Nikkei Architecture *and* Toshi Jutaku.

The residence is made up of two long pavilions set close together, forming an oblique angle that clearly separates the family accommodation from the guest quarters. At a break between the pavilions, two massive stone chimneys form a gateway allowing passage from the lush woods to the ocean frontage and directing entry into the house, creating a small intermediate patio. Both buildings have one storey. The larger pavilion, used by the family, is crossed horizontally by a third structure which marks the separation between the social and nighttime areas. The result is three separate volumes closely linked together.The family area starts at one end of the building with the living area around the hearth, followed by the dining room and kitchen in succession. The other wing, at the opposite end, houses a study and the bedrooms with en suite *bathrooms. The guest house is much smaller, and has its own bedrooms as well as a living/dining room and kitchen. Both buildings have a deck, more or less in the centre, commanding marvellous views.*

View of the spacious living room-dining room-kitchen, showing its clear and simple layout.

Structurally and formally, this house, by architect Peter Forbes, is a series of transverse bearing walls, carrying the roof deck. The walls are pierced by large and small openings to provide a continuous sequence of varied spaces. Free of any load bearing function, the exterior longitudinal walls are made entirely of sliding glass panels framed in teak and mahogany. This expanse of glass lets in a great deal of natural light, penetrating into every corner of the building. The few interior separating walls rarely reach the floor, and feature window-like openings giving continuity to the space. The almost total absence of doors eliminates all real physical barriers. The glass reflects the surroundings inside the house, metaphorically connecting the interior with the exterior.

All the interior and exterior surfaces are of different types of wood – cedar, mahogany and Douglas fir in various combinations and colours. This warm, beautiful material creates a very rustic and cosy atmosphere.

All of the furniture is wooden, even in the kitchen. The hearth is lined with stone, echoing the massive chimneys outside, and the span roof is covered with slate tiles.

The essential character of this roomy single-family dwelling by architect Peter Forbes is established by a series of simple geometrical forms and a clear and easily understood distribution of space. The architect has used a structure reminiscent of an unpretentious mountain refuge to skillfully achieve his principal objective: to introduce the spectacular surrounding landscape into the very rooms of the house, symbolically bringing man and his work closer to nature.

One of the main bedrooms opens onto a wooden deck overlooking the sea.

The master bedroom is visually connected with the coniferous forrest surrounding the house.

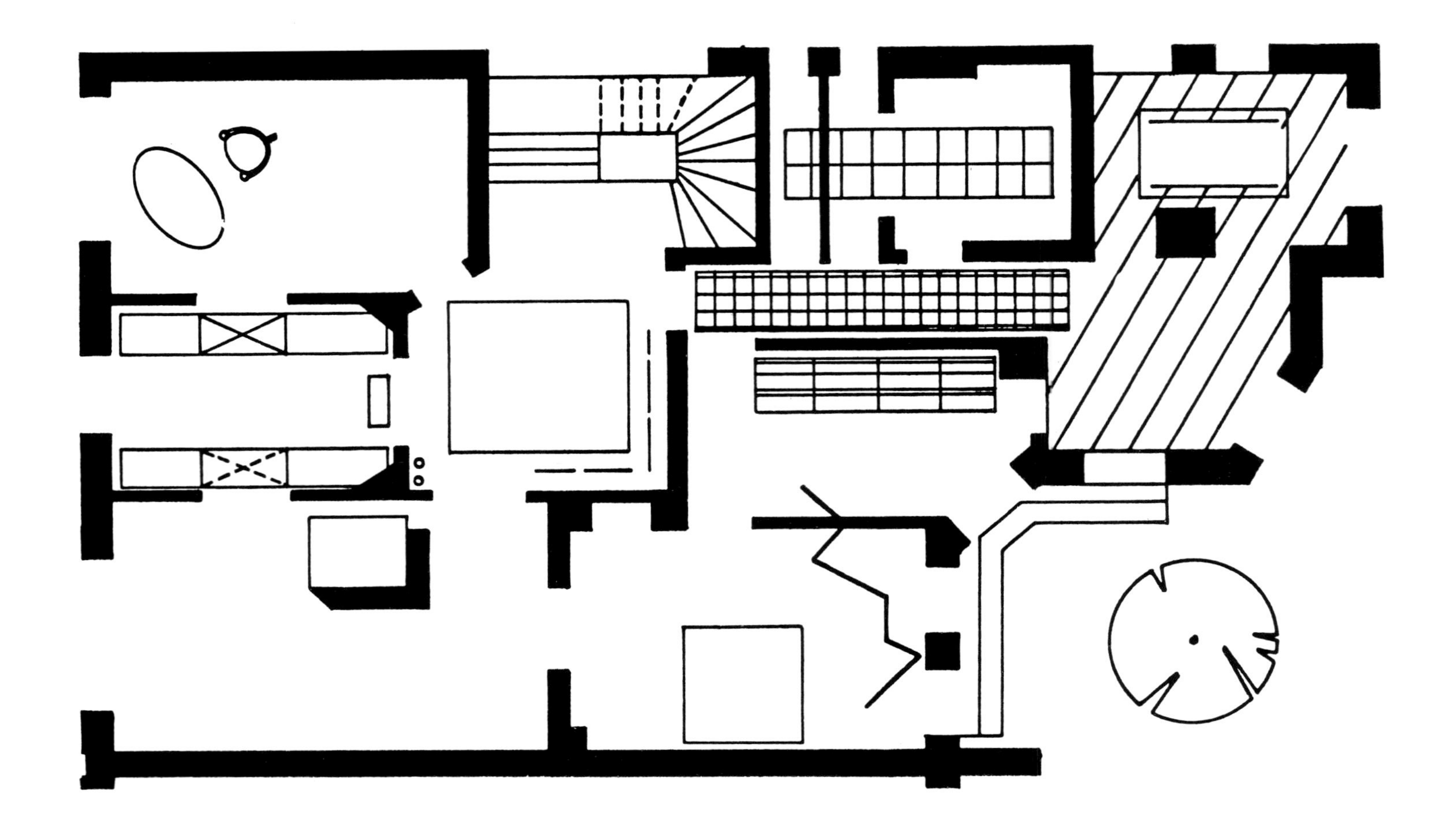

Floor plan.

Wohnung in Frankfurt

Norbert Berghof, Michael A. Landes and Wolfgang Rang

The desire to bring everyday life activities into a context where art is a dominant force has frequently occupied a great number of creative minds. The recent experiment by Norbert Berghof, Michael A. Landes and Wolfgang Rang falls within this sphere. The conceptual base bears a resemblance to the design carried out by Hans Posinger and the husband-and-wife team of Thommy-Kneschaurek of the Hotel Teufelhof in Basel, although with some differences of emphasis. The work by the architectural trio has been promoted on this occasion by Herbert Jopp. As the owner of an almost centennial building in one of the most characteristic sections of Frankfurt, Jopp decided to convert his own home into a centre for young German artists to put their ideas, inspired by the new tendencies, into practice.

Herbert Jopp broke with his sedentary life in Chicago to integrate himself in the tumultuous and rich cultural life of Frankfurt. To this end, he purchased the ground floor of a five-storey building, essentially of a traditional style, which dates back to 1903. It is located in one of the most revitalized areas, the western part of city.

This lower level had a surface area of 170 m^2 of usable space in an advanced stage of deterioration. It was only thanks to his work that part of the original splendour was regained. The ceilings throughout the apartment were restored using stucco and a bathroom was added. Here we must distinguish between the work necessary for construction and remodelling, and the theoretical foundation that goes into the work. The former refers to the processes of reconstruction, organization and

View of the study.

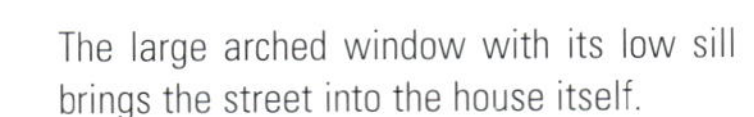

The large arched window with its low sill brings the street into the house itself.

distribution, not only of the interior, but of the facade, entrance and garden as well. The latter refers to the interior decoration and is at the suggestion of the promoter and owner, Herbert Jopp. The initial stage of the project consisted of architectural tasks which the firm Berghof, Landes and Rang handled. The first aspect of their job was to restore the support structures of the facade and to design the entryway and outdoor areas. The basic idea was to respect the traditional spirit of the structure, while introducing some innovations which would distinguish it from the adjacent buildings. Thus, for example, the low fence that separates the building from the street, as well as the beauty and the small scale of the garden, turn out to be surprising in their simplicity within the general urban environment. The exit from the north wing, which connects the library with the outdoors, was conceived by means of a slight grade, with careful workmanship of the Italian-inspired terrazzo, upon which one can perceive some of the motifs which will appear recurrently indoors: biomorphic fragments, such as a foot on a step – which translates the act of walking – or a hand on one of the banisters.

With respect to the original architecture, the most characteristic aspects have been enhanced, as in the case of the spectacular arched design of the openings in the facade, as well as the preservation of doors, frames, hinges and handles in the purest art nouveau style. The volume of the living space has a clearly prismatic shape, with relatively high ceilings (over three meters). Only one of the lateral sections had a somewhat irregular design. The

The furniture used in the dining room, as in the rest of the house, is strikingly modern in its design.

Strong colours are used to great effect without abandoning subtlety.

The lightness of the corridor that leads into the dining room is enhanced by the glass roof.

The bright bedroom gives directly on to the adjoining patio garden.

overall distribution of space has been maintained from the original.

The reception area embodies all the above themes to perfection. Upon leaving this area, one can move on to the library, the living room, the study and the corridor which leads to the remainder of the rooms. Another door conceals a small closet for shoes, although its real purpose is for the visible placement of drawers. The surface of the walls have been given a new look at the hand of Christian Appel with a pattern of intense and warm tonalities dominated by a reddish hue accented by yellow in the upper area. An invention of the trio of architects, the set of twin lamps, is made up of two highly stylized cylindrical columns (3.30 m) in terrazzo and gold, which culminate in two lamps directed at the ceiling. The existing oak floors have been preserved wherever possible; only the areas which suffered the most wear have been refinished. Only the kitchen, dining room, bathroom and lavatory have had their original workmanship substituted for a sober design in terrazzo. The doors, in general, have also been preserved, using frosted glass to maintain intimacy behind them.

The study and living room make up a single unified entity thanks to the presence of the library between them. An outstanding facet of the library is the placement of the most expressive examples of current tendencies in design upon the original wood surface.

The work of the architectural team, and their client, Herbert Jopp, have converted the ground floor of a solemn Frankfurt building into an outstanding example of a very specific tendency of contemporary design.

Although small, the toilet is decorated with flair in a slightly neoclassical style.

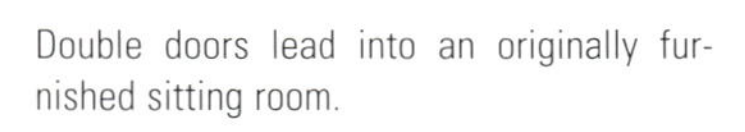
Double doors lead into an originally furnished sitting room.

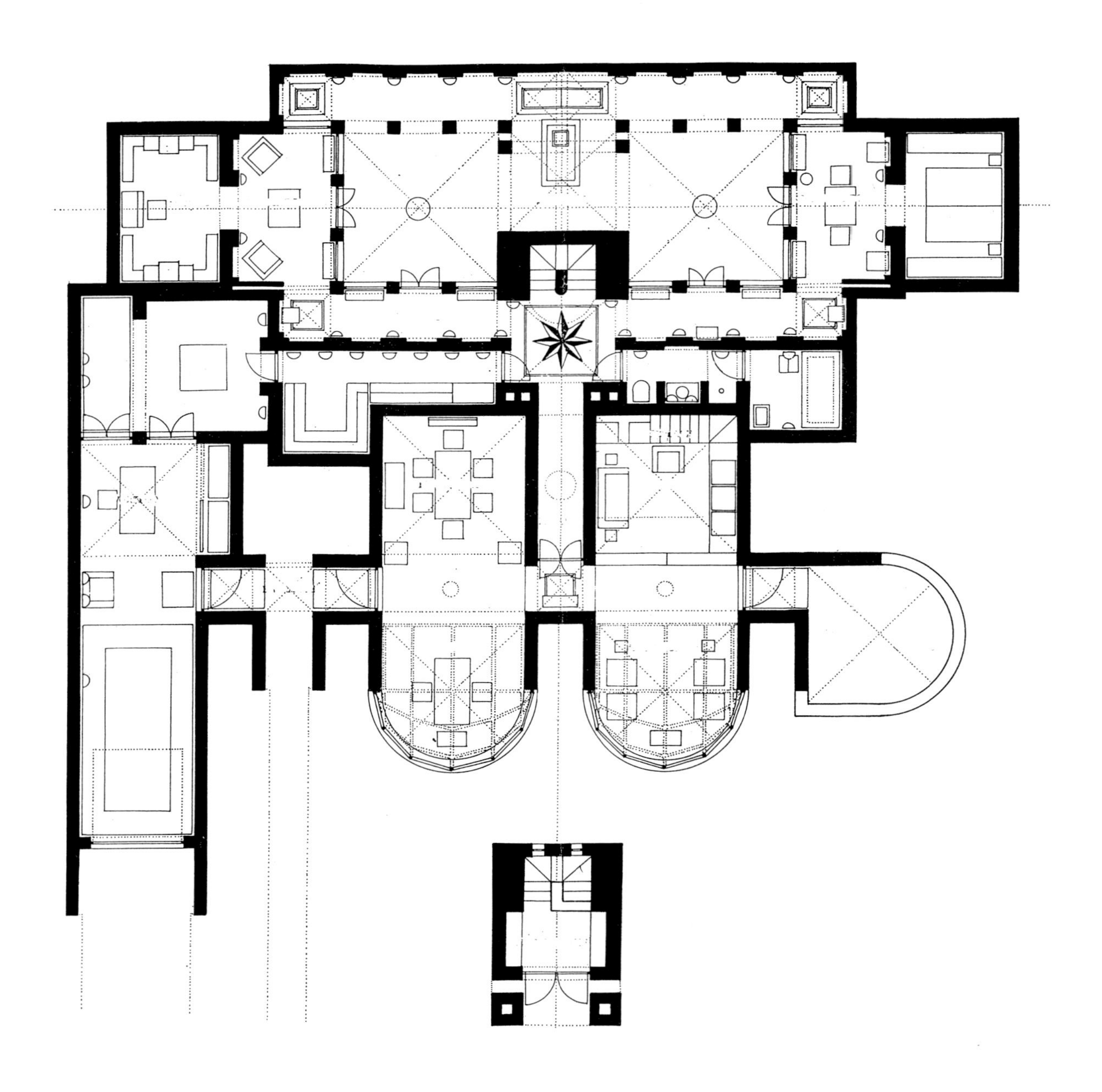

Plan of the different levels.

A hideaway among the dunes

Torsten Thorup & Claus Bonderup

For the architects Torsten Thorup and Claus Bonderup it was of utmost importance that this dwelling should form an integral part of the tense unity of the simple, dramatic surrounding landscape, becoming totally integrated into its setting. Therefore, the essential spirit and the individuality which distinguishes this house is expressed primarily in the layout and design of the interior.

This house is on the west coast of the Jutland peninsula in Denmark, set back from the sea, hidden among the sand dunes. The site has an undulating, irregular surface, and is completely covered with thick vegetation which conceals most of the building, shielding it from the eyes of curious passers-by. Its privileged situation and unusual layout afford the inhabitants of this house incredible views of the North Sea.

Torsten Thorup was born in Denmark in 1944. He studied Architecture and Planning in the Royal Academy of Fine Arts (1965-1969), and later, Psychology in the Faculty of Arts of the University of Copenhagen. After this, he did a master's in Architecture and Planning. His professional career began in 1963 when he worked with Bartoldy & Ohlsson Architects MAA in Copenhagen. Later, he worked with Westerby & Staer Architects MAA in the same city (1966) and Professor Henning Larsen, with whom he built various projects in Sweden in 1968. On his return to Denmark, he opened his own office together with the architect Claus Bonderup.

Claus Bonderup was born in Denmark in 1943. From 1965 to 1969 he studied Architecture and Planning at the Royal Academy of Fine Arts. Upon graduation, he began

The house is almost completely hidden, disguised by the thick vegetation and the undulations of the terrain itself.

working with Professor Henning Larsen in Copenhagen. He also worked with the architect Sergio Bernardes in Rio de Janeiro, Brazil (1970 to 1971), with Vischer & Weber in Basel, Switzerland (1971 to 1973), and with the office of Jacob Blegvad A/S in Aalborg, Denmark. Finally, he opened his own studio with Torsten Thorup in Copenhagen. They have built projects in association with Soeren Birch and Ellen Waade in Rovaniemi, Finland, and in Copenhagen. Their works, which have received several prizes and awards, are also displayed in the Museum of Modern Art and the Copper Hewlt Museum, both in New York.

The structure of this house is made up of a series of independent square forms of different sizes, giving rise to a complex and intricate sequence. The entire house is built on a single floor, so that the tower is the only element projecting above the construction.

On the left of the entrance, set in the seaward facade, there is a workroom open to the garage. These two areas form a prolongation of one end of the house. Turning towards the other side, the visitor comes to the only arched or circular volumetric spaces in the house, which contrast with the rectilinear forms. One of these spaces houses a rest and study area, and the other a sun lounge or summer dining room. At one end of the passageway that separates these rooms from the living room with a fireplace and the more sombre winter dining room, there is a semicircular terrace. A second corridor leads off at right angles to the kitchen, which has direct access to a patio. A large gallery separates these social areas from the

The circular volumes, which accommodate a rest and study area and summer dining room, contrast with the rectilinear forms.

private rooms, which are located at either end of this dividing line: to the right, the library and reading room, and on the opposite side, the morning room and a bedroom. All of these rooms are laid out around a beautiful atrium with a central fountain. The house also has a comfortable bathroom and a sauna.

Symmetry and geometry are the two continuous elements in the conception of this house designed by Torsten Thorup and Claus Bonderup. The construction of the different rooms is inspired by the simple lines of the cube and the circle, as seen in the living room, based on a square. The height of the room corresponds perfectly to its other dimensions, giving the whole a sense of equilibrium and proportion. At the same time, the classic vision of a city has dominated this architectural work as the underlying idea. The streets, market places and squares, each one a different size and character, all seem to be present in its layout. The passage from one room to another is always a fresh experience, arousing new emotions but nonetheless following a logical sequence.

The construction is almost completely hidden and disguised by the thick vegetation and the undulations of the dunes. In fact, from the exterior, only the ponderous, enclosed shape of the tower and the two clear geometrical glass forms are visible; the glass forms looking like two superhuman eyes set into the land itself.

The two architects considered it essential that the strong light coming off the sea should be fully appreciated from inside the rooms, and likewise that the sky and the view of the surrounding sand dunes should be enjoyed. As

The interior of one of the glassed spaces housing the study.

A detail of one of the glass structures with its arched roof looking like a cupula, clearly reminiscent of a geodesic dome.

is well known, the North Sea light has been admired for centuries by painters from all over Scandinavia for its truly unique character. This is why one of the chief aims of this project was to make the utmost use of the infinite possibilities of this characteristic light.

At the rear, the house is completely invisible; it opens onto a hollow in the sand, which, being buried among the dunes, is protected from the wind and inclement weather. This hollow, surrounded by a colonnade, is a small oasis, a garden overflowing with life, flowers and plants, sharply contrasting with the rough and rugged appearance of the surrounding dunes. All of the private rooms are wisely oriented towards this courtyard, preserving the privacy of the inhabitants.

The two circular forms housing the summer dining room and the study have arched ceilings like original, almost spherical cupolas, clearly reminiscent of a geodesic design. The key decorative elements here are the plants, which establish a clear link with the natural world outside, making the rooms resemble twin greenhouses.

In the centre of the building, there is a star painted on the floor, evoking the points of the compass, pointing in the thirty-two directions marked on the horizon.

The house is built of in-situ concrete and painted in a colour that echoes the sand of the natural setting into which the house is integrated in an almost spontaneous way. This decorative scheme gives it a warm and friendly character in the strong daylight.

Refuge and oasis by day, lighthouse by night when the glass forms are illuminated, this dwelling based on simple

Perspective of the corridor connecting the different areas of the house.

The garden, overflowing with plants, contrasts strongly with the rough, rugged surrounding terrain.

forms, such as the cube and the circle, built by the architects Torsten Thorup and Claus Bonderup, is concealed among the dunes and the vegetation covering them, integrating itself in a natural way into the splendour of the surrounding landscape. However, this subordination is only apparent because the interior forcefully reveals the distinctive identity of the house – singular and full of life.

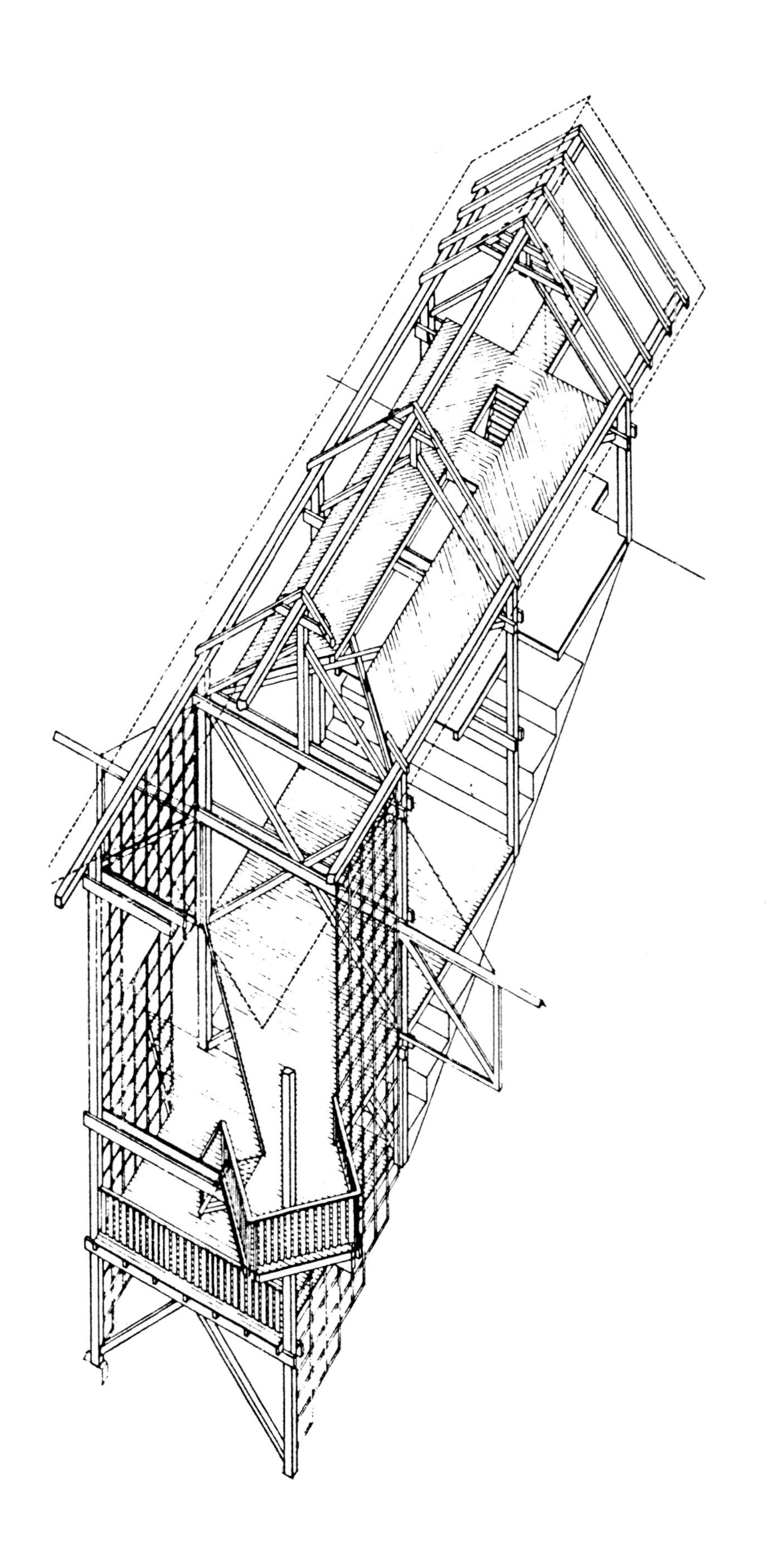

Axonometrc view of the house.

Traditional construction with new forms

Manfred Kovatsch

This single-family dwelling was originally designed as a holiday home, and is twenty minutes by car from Villach, Carinthia (Austria). It was built 350 metres above Lake Ossiach on terrain sloping sharply down to the water's edge. Its raised location provides sweeping views of the marvellous landscape surrounding the building on all sides. On a clear day the distant Karawanken mountains are visible.

Manfred Kovatsch was born in Austria in 1940. He studied at the Technical University in Graz, Austria, and here he came into contact for the first time with the world of construction. He later travelled to America and studied at the State University of California in Berkeley, where he obtained his degree in architecture. After graduation he worked in association with other architects on a number of projects, and also taught many classes as associate lecturer at the Technical University in Munich, Germany. Since 1986 he has been a professor of the Fine Arts Academy in Munich, where he now lives. His built work is now extremely prolific and the source of much admiration. This is borne out by the fact that his design won a prize in 1991 for a council residences project. This project was begun in 1977, but was delayed for a number of years while building permission was granted, and for this reason construction work did not actually start until the beginning of the eighties.

This single-family dwelling was built on a slightly irregular but also slightly rectilinear ground plan, and consists of four separate levels wedged into a wooden supporting framework like the various decks of a ship. A

Side view of the house from the approach, with a partial view of lake Ossiach to the right.

number of stairways, of differing lengths due to the slope of the building, are the main supporting features. The staircase on the valley elevation takes in all four levels, and that on the ravine elevation takes in only two. Manfred Kovatsch managed to put the sloping terrain to good use. Thus, on top of the base – a framework of wooden beams connected to the foundations above ground level – he built a set of wide steps leading up to the dwelling. These steps have a dual role since, on the one hand, they can be used for rest and relaxation during periods of fine weather and, on the other, their hollow inside can be used for storage. An exterior staircase leads up to the second floor, containing the main terrace and the living room area. This covered terrace is used as an outdoor relaxation spot, and is a kind of triangular balcony/booth whose base is exactly half that of the square floor plan. The third level, built into the hillside, contains the dining room and the kitchen, which juts out pulpit-like towards the lounge area. Finally, the top floor houses one bedroom with several beds, in addition to a large bathroom and WC. Another peculiarity of the south facade is that when the sliding glass door closes, its sloping supports line up with the diagonal shoring on the support construction. This is a most obvious transparent construction, since it provides unimpeded views of the ceiling.

Manfred Kovatsch's structure is really quite simple, and stems from the premise of some extremely simple ideas which allowed the main framework to be erected in only three days. The staircases were fastened securely to the ground by a series of bars, and then the architect proceeded to build the roof and the walls around this. A large, diagonal crossbar gives rigidity to this system of stairways and double ties.

The owners of this residence had chosen to live amid natural surroundings, adapting these surroundings to the construction materials, and also to construction methods which would respect the setting, the vegetation and the animals on the property. There is simply no comparison between life in a wooden mountainside refuge and life in a cold city apartment. One of the magical features of this particular dwelling is that somehow it lives and grows alongside the occupants in continual evolution.

One of the common objectives of both the architect and the owners was to make the building shine out in some natural way. The roof, which slopes sharply on both sides as protection against inclement weather, was the best element to start with in such a case. Its silvery-grey colour under sunlight contrasts with a swamp-like grey in bad weather conditions, and this only enhances the appearance of the building as part of the surroundings. Moreover, the planks of larch wood and sheets of spruce on the basic wooden framework create a yellowish shade and a golden-brown colour which contrast with the green of wood and meadow.

Manfred Kovatsch managed to combine the artistic with the functional in this construction. The perspex hatch windows open by traction on a weighted cable. Macrolon cladding fitted with an air valve protects the

Detail of the terrace on the upper level.

Detail of the ground floor interior.

View of the interior from the stairway leading to the bedrooms.

Interior detail of the bedrooms on the upper level, with the bath tub and tap arrangement in the foreground.

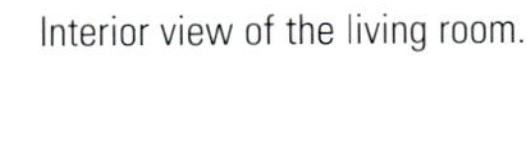

Detail of the kitchen on the ground floor.

Interior view of the living room.

pulpit against the wind. Kovatsch also designed the cylindrical Canadian oven with its system of hot air conduits. This Bullerjan almost suppresses the need for electrical heating. Another source of heat is the sun coming in through the south facade at approximately 25° on a hot day. All this makes for a restful, cheerful ambience – the frameless windows, for example. The seats and chairs were specially made by a master carpenter from a design worked out by the architect and the owner of the house.

This house by Manfred Kovatsch and the surrounding landscape create new shapes and new lifestyles in such a way that traditional and modern features, rationality and decoration are brought together in a house bursting with memories and reminiscence, which nevertheless avoids any rustic sentimentality. This is basically a holiday home which respects the traditions of the area, and it is a unique construction as regards its shape. Thus it is no mere replica, but a truly original structure whose creator has once again understood the message of the surroundings and has built a house for this particular client who wanted to live among the trees. Careful study and analysis of the design reflect the qualities of this unusual residence – gracefulness, simplicity and creativity.

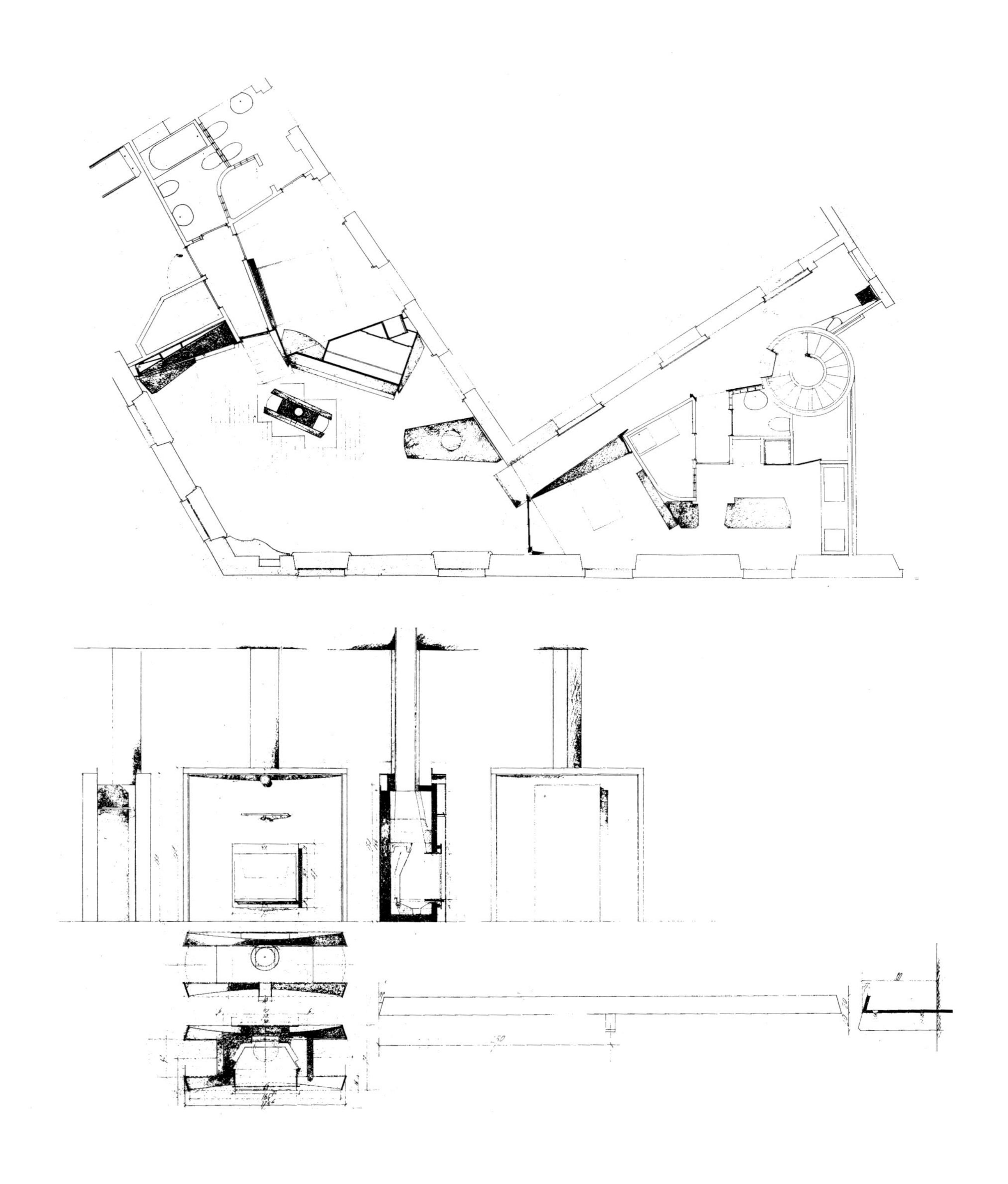

Plan of the lower level and various sections of the fireplace.

Casa Insinga

Umberto Riva

The Milanese architect Umberto Riva, with his particular affinity for themes that are usually considered minor or secondary, demonstrates through this interior organization of an existing structure on the Via Arena in Milan the exceptional power of his creative style. This is a brilliant exercise in the interpretation of the physical characteristics of an apartment whose only expressive element is the disposition of openings. In taking on this project, Riva did not hesitate to explore the architectural theories on the renovation process and arrived at the conclusion that, in such an awkward setting, the most reasonable solution was to ignore all of the current stereotypes and create a language that would offer a personal approach to the rehabilitation process.

In this case, his fundamental break with convention consisted in granting one of the most frequently neglected areas of a residence – the corridor – the key function of the living space. The interior was designed with an eye to movement, and a natural circulation pattern was established based on the free-flowing sequences and perspectives that determine its dynamic image. To achieve this, there are no obstacles or physical boundaries, the distribution being defined by non-structural elements (the table, the fireplace and the flooring).

This regular placement of the openings is the most expressive motif of the apartment, and the layout takes the utmost advantage of the transparency they offer. The usable living area consisted of two intersecting trapezia with differences in both the orientation and in the size of their smaller sides, which resulted in wasted space and

A whole wall of wood in the bedroom is used to house fitted cupboards.

The approach to the decoration was to use warm yet light tones.

The kitchen (background) and dining room (foreground) are partly separated.

The spiral staircase, in unfaced masonry, unlike the rest of the house.

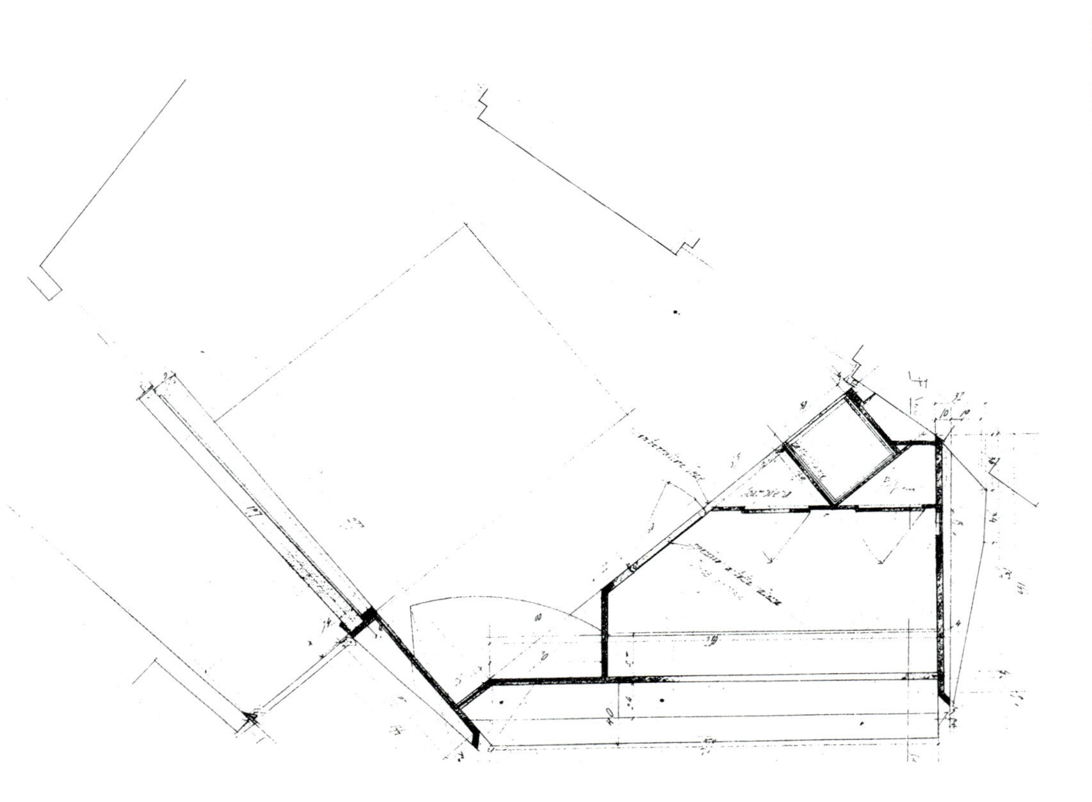

Plan of the upper floor.

The entrance hall and corridor, with a coat-rack and the bulge of the spiral staircase on the left.

angular corners that were difficult to use. Another determining aspect of this highly irregular floor plan was the location of the entrance in one of the corners of the smaller trapezoidal space. On the positive side, the apartment has a magnificent terrace that overlooks the courtyard.

With these inconvenient volumetric characteristics as the point of departure, the Milanese architect introduced a domestic programme which made it eminently livable. The physical aspects called for an out-of-the-ordinary layout, based on two key concepts that distance this intervention from the mainstream. Firstly, no architectural conventions were employed in the design beyond the most basic functional elements, and these were adapted to the specific nature of the existing volume. Secondly, he did not impose his own individuality on the space and its programme; on the contrary, his personal affinities were subordinate to the requirements of the intervention.

In short, the two basic tenets of the plan were the rejection of traditional hierarchy and the promotion of interior movement. Each of these principles would act in an independent but complementary manner to create a new interior reality that takes maximum benefit of the apartment's natural light and establishes sufficiently spacious areas appropriate to the household's activities.

A conventional articulation of the functional programme could not be carried out in such an irregular volume. The architect had to ignore those formulas that emphasized the importance of isolated, independent rooms. For an apartment governed by straight lines and angles that

General view of the living room, dominated by the huge freestanding fireplace.

View vertically down the stairwell, showing the variety of textures.

Detail of the living room, with the dining room in the background.

The fireplace is very much the focus of the lower level of the house.

The rear of the fireplace, showing the chromatically differentiated recessed sides.

continually changed direction, Riva chose to grant special significance to the corridor. Thus he designed a logical circulation pattern that begins at the entrance and, running parallel to the partition wall of the smaller trapezium, leads to the terrace connected to the large living room.

The corridor thus serves the functions of communication and distribution and favours the second objective by imbuing the visual reading of the interior with a dynamic character. The concept of movement is dramatised by this natural circulation route that offers the apartment a continuity of perspective. In this way, it is impossible to view the space as a static, unitary and complete area that does not respond in any sense to the volumetric features of the premises. The visual reading is based on the corridor, which has been transformed into a series of richly expressive sequences, of partial views and scattered fragments that are drawn into a unity by the material treatment, the use of colour and the natural light, as well as by its harmonious atmosphere.

To achieve these purposes it was necessary to avoid, insofar as possible, any architectural barriers that would act as obstacles to the process of perception. However, the itinerary had to be designed and delimited. For this Riva employed a minimum of structural elements, allocating the demarcation functions to various other types of components. He rejected the standard device of the partition wall, aiming for an economy of planes and gestures and fostering the penetration and diffusion of light from the numerous windows. Two partition walls were deemed sufficient. The first, in the smaller trapezium

View across the lower floor from the kitchen to one of the living room windows.

Main door and entrance hall, featuring the coatrack-cum-umbrella stand.

space, establishes the separation between the corridor leading to the living room and the less public areas of that volume (the kitchen and the bathroom). The second partition divides the living room from the bedrooms and bathrooms of the larger trapezoid.The curved section of the partition at the beginning of the corridor repeats the cylindrical development of the stairway, with its inner surface faced in brick and the sumptuous plastic form of the steps. Another of the dominant aspects of the apartment is the attention focused on the openings, on the views of the urban setting and on the transparency of the interior. The spacious, luminous interior atmosphere is emphasized by the use of wooden furniture, an honest, warm material that is well-suited to the creative work of the Milanese architect.

In short, Umberto Riva's intervention in this apartment on the Via Arena in Milan is a magnificent exercise in spatial distribution, with an economy of expression that seeks to reorder a ground plan that was as inconvenient as it was attractive. To accomplish this, he had to look beyond the more conventional models of residential works, and grant a leading role to one of the least significant elements of the programme, the corridor. By this means, the appearance is no longer static and unitary, but rather a rich series of visual sequences and fragments, governed by the idea of movement. Regarding the work as a whole, the architect has successfully achieved his objectives, which implied foregoing the pretensions of the 'artist/architect' although the interior mood is imbued with his unique creative vision.

This building is, to a certain extent, a variation on the strong cubist forms.

Sketch of the house.

Connection with protection

Steven Ehrlich

This recent work by architect Steven Ehrlich springs from his intuition about the feelings and taste in houses of the future owners; their idea of a home. The design for this small urban beach house, whose front patio is a beautiful Pacific beach, is based on an unusual modernist idea that aims to connect the interior and the exterior without sacrificing the protection and security of the inhabitants.

This single-family dwelling faces Santa Monica beach in the city of Los Angeles, California. Set on a small site practically on the beach, the house is built in an area between the Pacific Coast highway and a beach-front promenade which runs along the white ocean sands. Despite the spatial limitations, the design takes full advantage of the fantastic views of the ocean.

Born in New York City in 1946, Steven Ehrlich studied Architecture at Rensselaer Polytechnic Institute in New York. In 1969, after graduating, he enlisted in the Peace Corps and was sent to work in Marrakech, Morocco for the Moroccan Office of Planning and Housing from 1969 to 1971. The following year, he travelled in north and west Africa, absorbing the indigenous culture and architecture. In 1973, he returned to America and built three houses in Vermont. But the call of Africa led him to return to Nigeria, where he taught Architecture in the Ahmadu Bello University in Zaria. He also built a theatre-workshop in Zaria, combining Western construction technologies with traditional local materials, such as mud, thatch and bamboo, in a moving fusion of contrasting imagery.

Upon returning to the United States, Ehrlich looked for aesthetic correlatives for the vital African simplicity in contemporary American architecture. He found echoes of this influence in the work of Louis Kahn and in some of the periods of Rudolph Schindler, as well as in the strong, clear forms of the proto-modernist Irving Gill and the classical modernism of Le Corbusier. He decided to settle in Los Angeles because of the raw energy of this city, its connection to nature and its cultural diversity. He opened his own office in Venice, California in 1979. His maturity as an architect suggests a tough-minded idealism, and his built work is made up of distinctive buildings characterised by a well-defined and highly personal style.

This building, constructed on a rectangular base, is 45 feet high and only 18 feet wide, divided into three and a half levels. The ground or access floor houses the entrance, in the central part of the building. There is a garage on one side, which can accommodate several vehicles, and a guest bedroom with private bath on the other side. The stairway in the hall leads to the first floor. This floor houses the kitchen, connected to a dining room in the centre of the space and to a living room that gives onto the exterior terrace. The whole floor is a single immense open-plan space, which serves as a two-level social area for family life. The mezzanine intermediate level serves as a sort of parenthesis between this floor and the nighttime area on the top floor. This floor

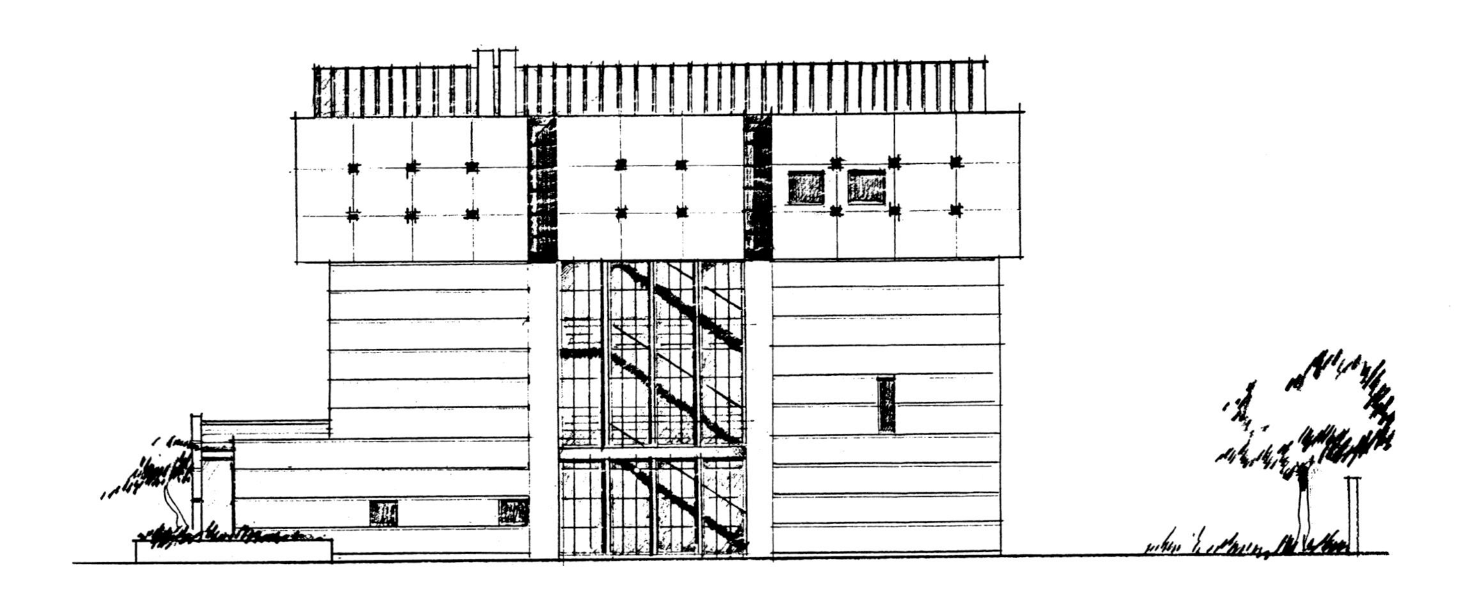

Section of the house.

Section of the house.

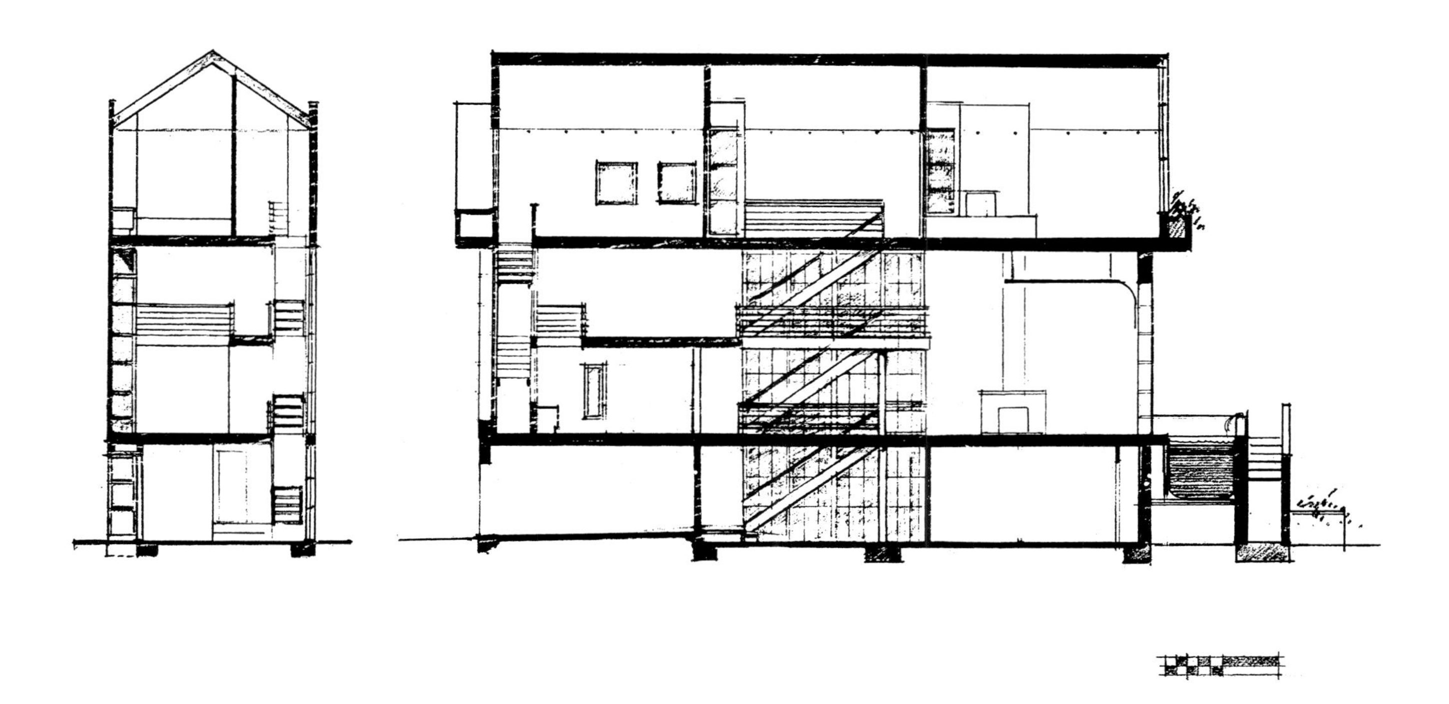

includes the children's bedroom and a master suite which opens onto a balcony. Both of the bedrooms have en suite *bathrooms.*

Steven Ehrlich defines himself as an "architectural anthropologist" who observes the connections between social traditions, climate and construction techniques in different cultures.

In this design the author wanted to create an effective fusion between the interior and the exterior, a characteristic feature of southern Californian dwellings. However, he took great pains to not overexpose the inhabitants to the powerful natural environment around the dwelling.

Modern technology, in the form of a broad 16-foot-high sectional glass door that rolls up completely to the ceiling was used to eliminate any physical barrier between the living room and outdoors.

Softly translucent materials let natural light into the house from all sides, while also maintaining a distance between the inhabitants and the less interesting urban environment around the house. Thus, Ehrlich lets the landscape become a part of daily life without going so far as to allow it to infringe on or interfere with domestic tranquility. Ehrlich defines himself as a "regionalist", capable of responding to the particular character of a setting with a deeply specific response.

This building is, to a certain extent, a variation on the strong cubist forms whose tensions are restfully resolved within their own aesthetic means. The work also displays the author's talent for contriving volumes whose

A more closed rear facade made of concrete withdraws and separates the house from the urban environment.

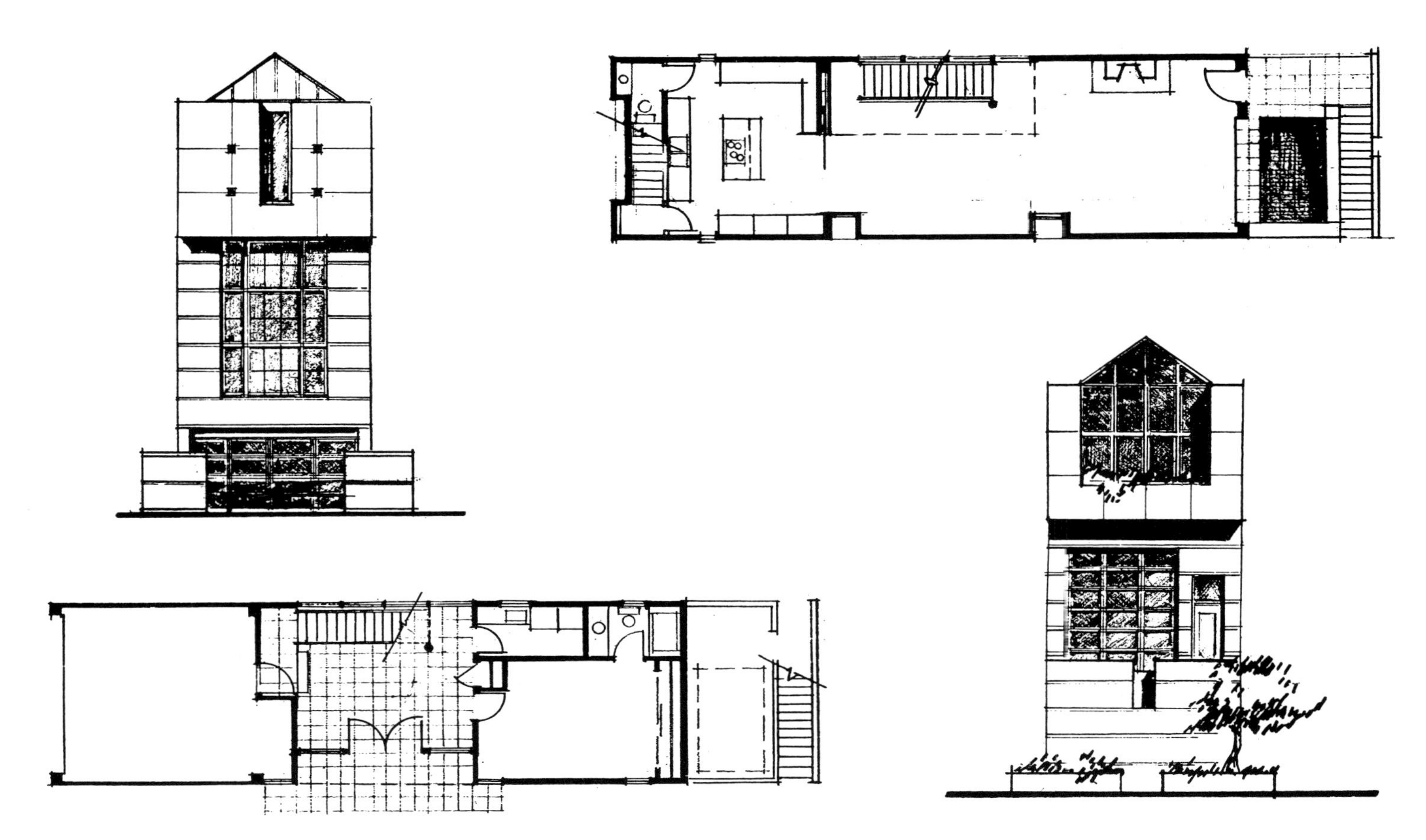

Elevations of the house.

Plans of the different levels.

1273

A detail of the functional stairway leading to the first floor.

Perspective of the stairway with carpeted steps.

Wooden furniture contrasts with modern designs.

Large windows connect the living room with the terrace, sand and sea.

Living area of the upper floor with designer furniture and smooth walls.

proportions of height, length and breadth resolve the energies they contain. As in the Kalfus studio and the Vining-Doughty house, this design juxtaposes large expanses of wall, treated as a sculptural mass, with large areas of glass, creating an impressive cubic form with glass walls. In fact, this skeletal, block-like structure recalls the "primitive" structures which Steven Ehrlich so admired in Africa.

At the top of the stairway which leads up from the living room, a hanging landing leading to a loft functions as a suspended bridge – as at the Miller-Nazarey residence – giving a sensation of lightness and volatility.

The windows and doors have very diverse geometric forms (rectangles, pentahedrons, and squares) creating interesting interplays of light and shadow.

The concrete outside walls combine a bluish-grey hue with a light earth colour, which harmonises perfectly with the ever-changing blue of the ocean and the soft whiteness of the sandy beach.

The square blocks and horizontal bands that form the structure of the walls give the building a cubic geometrical aspect, reflected inside in the fireplace, also created by adding bands. The floors inside the house are covered either with parquet, as in the kitchen and bathroom, or with ceramic tiles. Pieces of more traditional wooden furniture contrast with the modern designs in chairs and tables.

Steven Ehrlich's faith in the modernist slogan "form follows function", coined by Louis Sullivan and popularised by Ludwig Miës Van der Rohe, as a

The double height social area for family life.

Interior of the bathroom showing the juxtaposition of the geometric forms of the bath and shower unit.

profoundly intuitive response to the symbolic and emotional demands of architectural integrity, is the basis of this single-family dwelling on Santa Monica beach. This house, which reflects the ability to be at once highly ingenious and completely simple, both energetic and serene, is a space in perfect equilibrium between the sophisticated and the innocent, the civilised and the primitive. By creating total communication between the landscape and the architectural work without diminishing the security and privacy of the occupants, Steven Ehrlich manages to reconcile the desire for emotional security – a place of perfect rest – with a feeling of compressed intensity.

View of the living room from the kitchen.
The floors are covered with parquet.

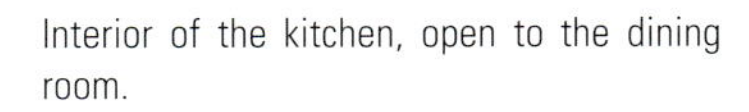

Interior of the kitchen, open to the dining room.

The horizontal bands of the exterior are echoed in the hearth area. The chimney flue is made of glass.

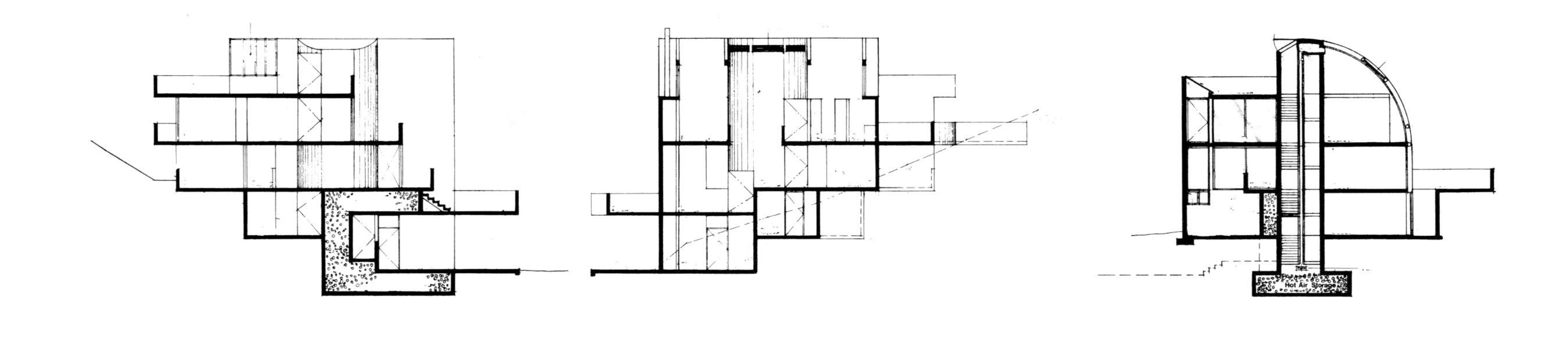
Hot Air Storage

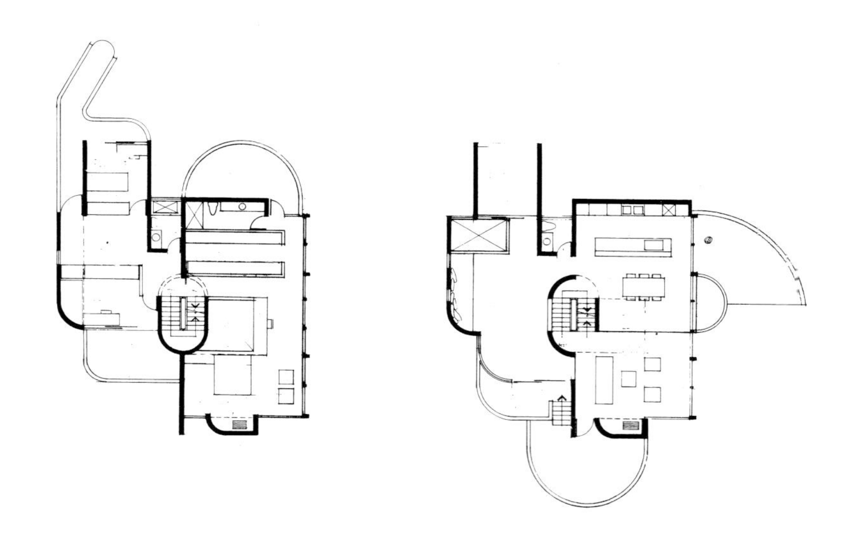

Sections of the house.

Plans of the various floors.

Floor plan.

Towards kinetic architecture

Ray Kappe

Most of Ray Kappe's hillside constructions are connected to the landscape horizontally. Cookston House, however, has a vertical connection in concrete and a castle-like structure, and is both surrounded and covered by trees. It is a particularly unusual construction for the Rustic Canyon area, and was sited to take advantage of flat terrain used for a long entrance path.

Other houses are bordered by roads, but Ray Kappe's house seems to be literally stuck to acres of marvellous countryside and only linked to the road by a large door made of concrete, steel and glass.

The original design was for an Iranian couple with two small children who wished to live in a concrete building with round forms and shapes. Kappe took advantage of these circumstances to build a very different structure from previous projects which have won him architectural renown. To this end, his main inspiration stemmed from energy-saving and energy research criteria.

Ray Kappe is an architect, designer and teacher of international repute, who has been working as a professional architect in Los Angeles since 1953. He founded the SCI-ARC (Southern California Institute of Architecture in Los Angeles), and also introduced the Vico Morcote programme in Switzerland. He was director of this initiative for fifteen years.

In 1985 he established the Kappe Architects Planners practice in Santa Monica, Los Angeles, in association with Herbert Kahn, Rex Lotery and Cleio Boccato. Some of the built work carried out by this partnership in Los Angeles includes: the master plan for the Watts Community Arts

Partial view of one of the upper level balconies.

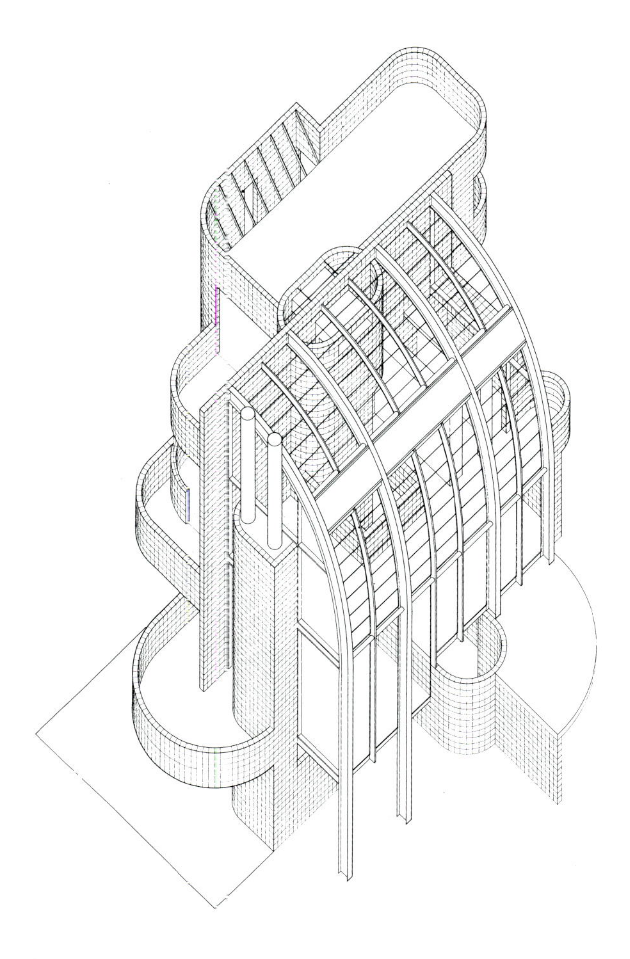

Axonometric view.

Detail of one of the facades, on a partial view of the glass arch.

View of the entrance facade.

Center, Ramona Gardens, an office block in Beverly Hills, the master plan, design and construction of the Beverly Hills Corporation Yard and Community Center and the administration building for the Santa Monica bus network.

The combination of round roof structures, projecting balconies and a curved bridge to the rear of the wall creates a composition contrast beside the all-glass south facade. This structure is divided along its north-south axis by a wall running from west to east, and despite the fact that the formal composition was determined by energy-related criteria, the building rises up majestically within its setting and provides views of the area around the canyon.

This house was planned during the oil crisis and the installation of the new government in Iran, and both these factors exerted their influence on the final construction. In this work, Kappe uses both active and passive systems in response to California's energy regulations. He wished to create living space which would be viable as far as energy was concerned, without however forfeiting a lifestyle befitting the southern Californian climate. Thus he attempted to use large glass surfaces to draw sunlight towards both the interior and the exterior of the dwelling. The entire glassed-in south facade is protected whenever necessary by a movable shutter.

The house functions as a passive collector of solar energy, and uses the block of concrete and the concrete on the other floors for increased thickness.

All the warm air collected during the day and kept in a storeroom made from rock is used to warm the house at night for eight hours. The air is collected on the upper

Partial view of the kitchen/dining room.

section of the southern elevation, is wafted through to the rock storeroom and distributed around the house when the temperature drops. Solar collectors in the walls on the south facade provide a source of hot water, and also act as a backup to the passive system, thus saving the owners more money.

Inside the house, the effect of spaciousness from the entrance level to the top level is enhanced by the opening between the levels. This also enhances the verticality of the structure and provides exquisite views of the nearby eucalyptus tree and the hilltop beyond.

The Iranian revolution, which was taking place during construction work on this building, was to have unlucky consequences for the original owners. The basic shell was built, and the unfinished residence waited several years for a new set of owners. The Cookston family bought the house, and it was finished by the same architect. They were keen to monitor and reorganise the environment, and so even more innovative features were added to this unusual dwelling. The original plan for a computer-controlled thermostat system was extended to include a system to control the lights, the water sprinklers, the security system, etc. Sensors were placed around the house to monitor changes in the environment and to comply with environmental regulations. For two years Ray Kappe was involved in the development of a kinetic computer-controlled environmental monitoring system. He then began to design a house for NASA using transfer technology. Thanks to the Cookston, it is possible that kinetic systems may one day become a common feature of most residences.

Interior view of the kitchen/dining room.

Interior view of a corridor.

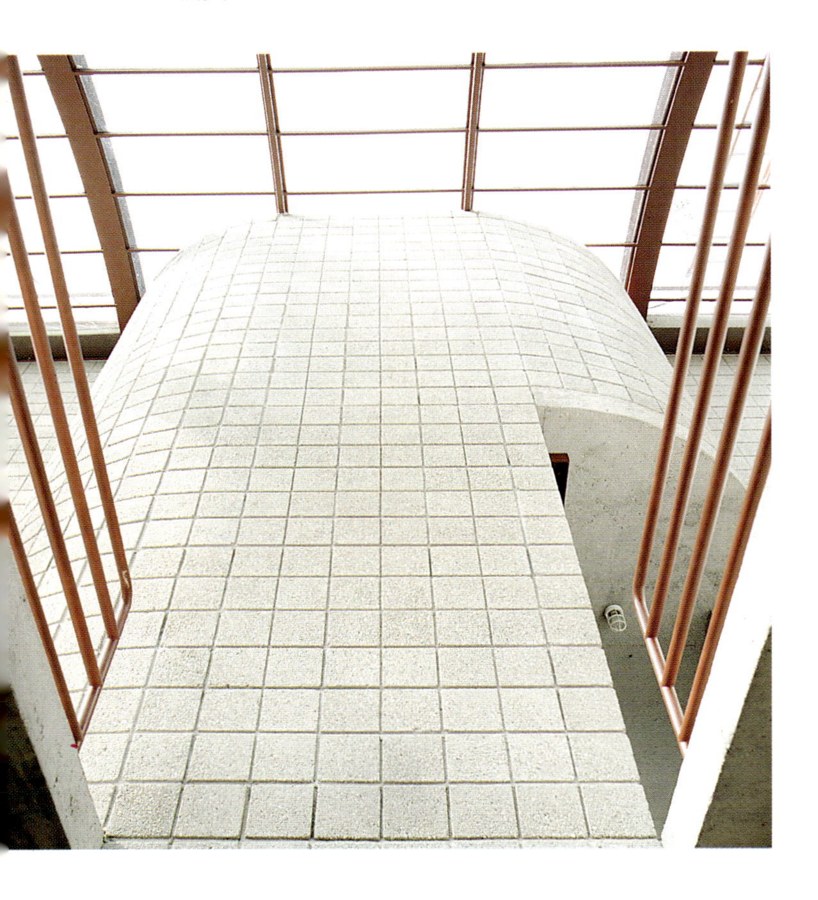

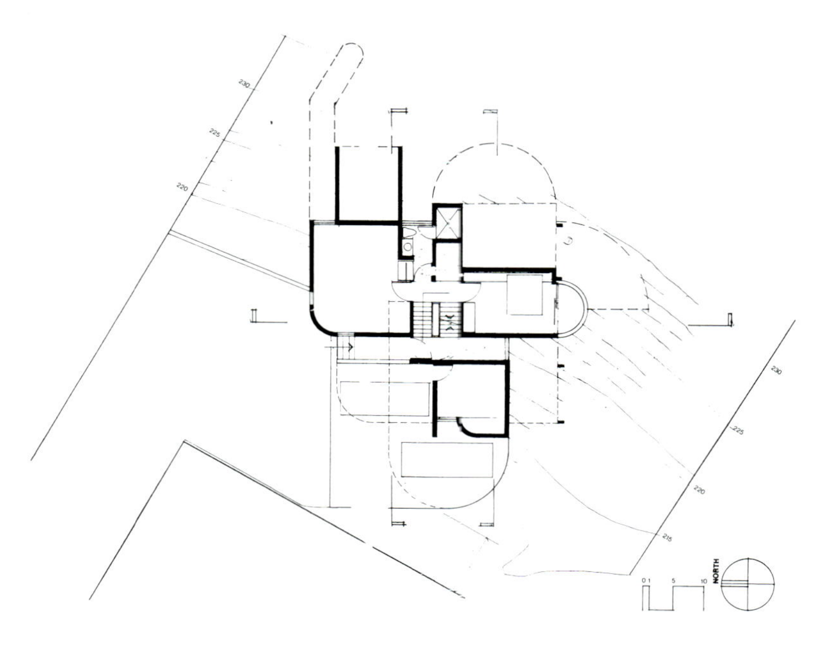

The interior consists of large open spaces, cosily interconnected between the various floors. The central stairway and the clearly visible mechanical mounting develop the building vertically and also horizontally, ending with a platform which offers a view of the area around the canyon on all sides. The stairway is red metal and the steps were made from a transparent material. This entire area is brightened by the large glass structure on the south facade.

The interior decoration follows the same guidelines of comfort, simplicity and elegance. However, the most original element is the main bedroom located in the curved glass structure. It is spacious, and was executed in glass and concrete. The bed is situated in the centre of the room, and provides a view of the landscape around the canyon.

Thus the Cookston House in Los Angeles by Ray Kappe is an example of a change in his style. It is a vertical building with extremely different facades: a castle-like structure, a mélange of solid constructions – balconies, and so on – on the north elevation and curved glassed-in south elevation containing the main bedroom, which is in close contact with nature and the surroundings and thus represents a break in the traditional conception of space. This beauty of form has one objective: saving energy by harnessing solar power, and this led the architect and the owners to carry out further investigation into the field of kinetics through a computerised system to monitor changes in the environment. The Cookston House crosses the frontiers of traditional architecture, availing itself of new systems and schools of thought geared more towards the future than the past.

Interior view of the living room, with the glass dining room unit in the background.

Detail of the interior staircase.

Interior view of the main bedroom within the spectacular glass structure providing a splendid vista of the canyon.

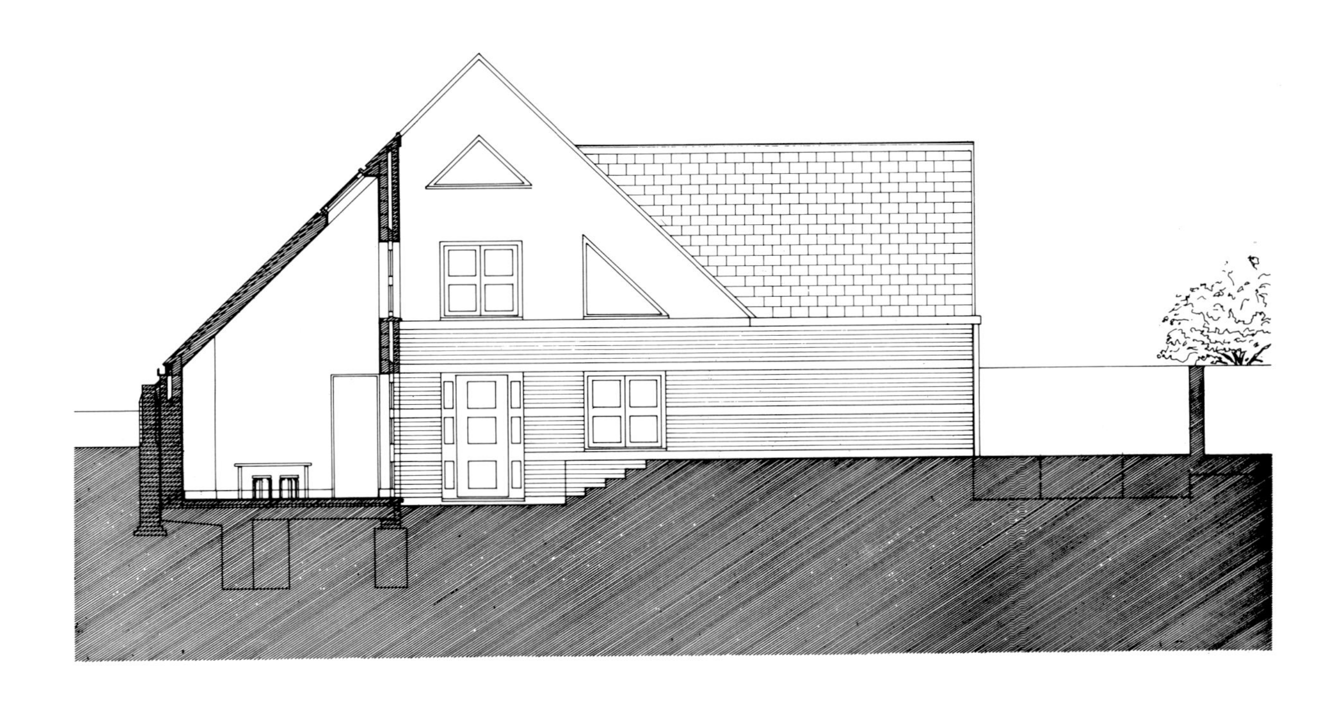

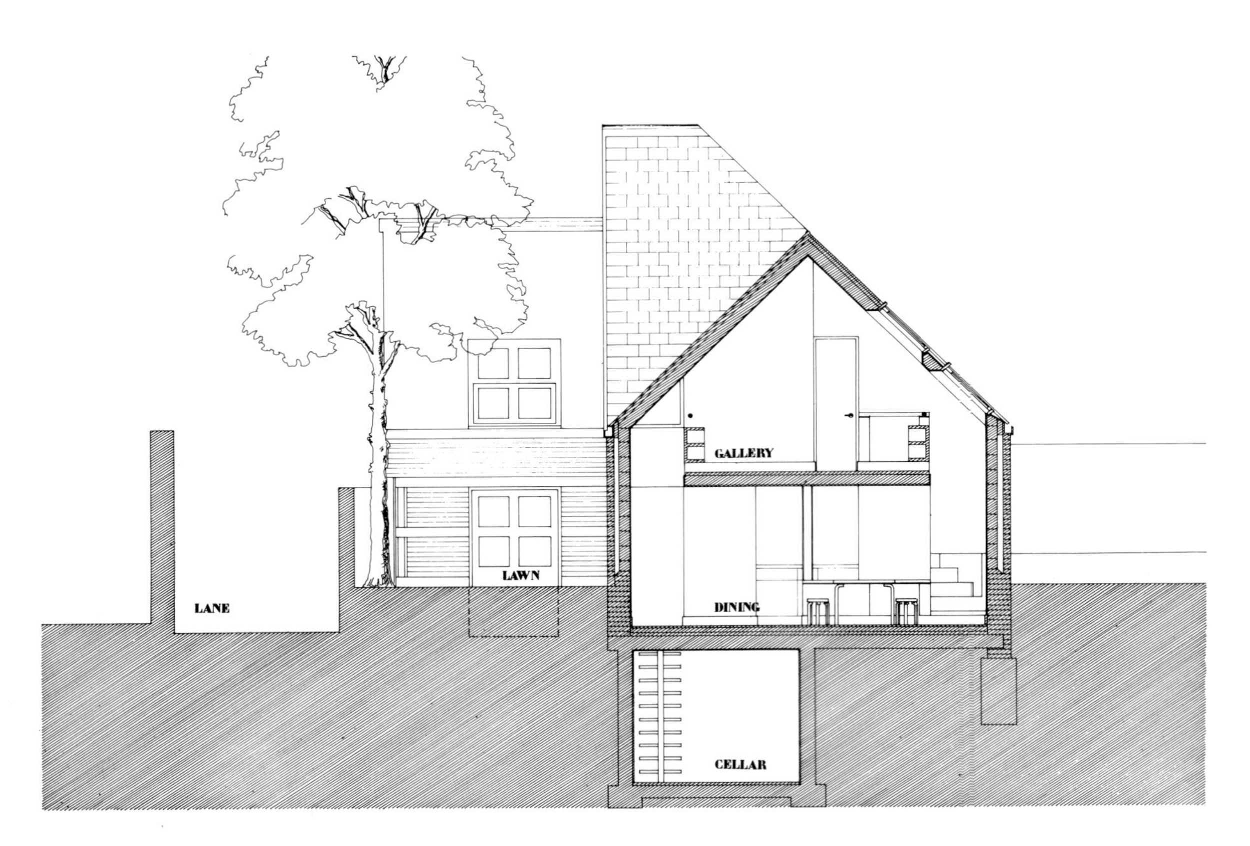
GALLERY
LAWN
LANE
DINING
CELLAR

Frontal section.

Lateral section.

Studio House

Martin Goalen

The relationship between the architect and his client is so ambiguous that it often interferes with the former's purposes while the latter's needs are left unfulfilled. When client and architect are one and the same person, the experience will undoubtedly constitute a stimulating exercise in which the objectives coincide with the results, the proposals with the achievements. In the case of Studio House, Martin Goalen has completed a magnificent project through which, in addition to further defining his elegant, austere style, he has entered the field of Cubist rationalism associated with the master Le Corbusier, transforming this interior into a work of explicit homage to the French architect, as well as an expansion of the limits of the abstract, logical vocabulary of the first half of the twentieth century.

The project as a whole is a work in which the external reality is as important as the internal. This is a paradigmatic example of the separate single-family house. However, its realization involved a number of factors that had a great influence on the definitive fabric. The house took six years to complete due to the constant modifications made in the design and to certain legal building restrictions. The result was a seemingly simple structure, which is nevertheless analytically and stylistically complex, with a highly visual and expressive quality.

The new construction is sited at the end of the large garden of a Victorian house (the property of the architect) located in one of the quietest districts in London. It was built in a side street, College Lane, a narrow road parallel to Highgate Road, the main traffic artery connecting the British capital with the northern suburb of Highgate. Until the nineteenth century, the urban development of this zone had been completely linear. Subsequently, a lateral growth took place and the original farms gave way to a network of streets with houses similar to the one being studied.

This context was the physical constraint on the site and, to a certain extent, on the typology of the new house. The L-shaped studio is positioned at the end of the garden of the architect's Victorian house, which faces Lady Somerset Road. The studio building has a narrow facade on College Lane and its appearance is enhanced by the row of old linden trees along the road.

Regarding the architectural setting, the basic building material is brick, softened by climbing ivy, and the variety of levels.

The project divided the site into three open-air spaces: the entrance courtyard; a strip of lawn that rises gently toward College Lane; and a small interior terrace on the lower level that faces the Victorian house. With this arrangement the ground plan of the studio/residence took the shape of an L, which clarified the distribution between the living and the service areas.

The exterior architecture reflects this simple tripartite spatial layout. However, the local authorities imposed several stipulations that influenced the formal aspect of the building. The angle of intersection between the

Detail of the frontage, taken from the lane, showing the top of the main gate and the variety of window shapes.

View across the dining room from the front door, with the way through to the kitchen on the left.

Ground plan of the property.

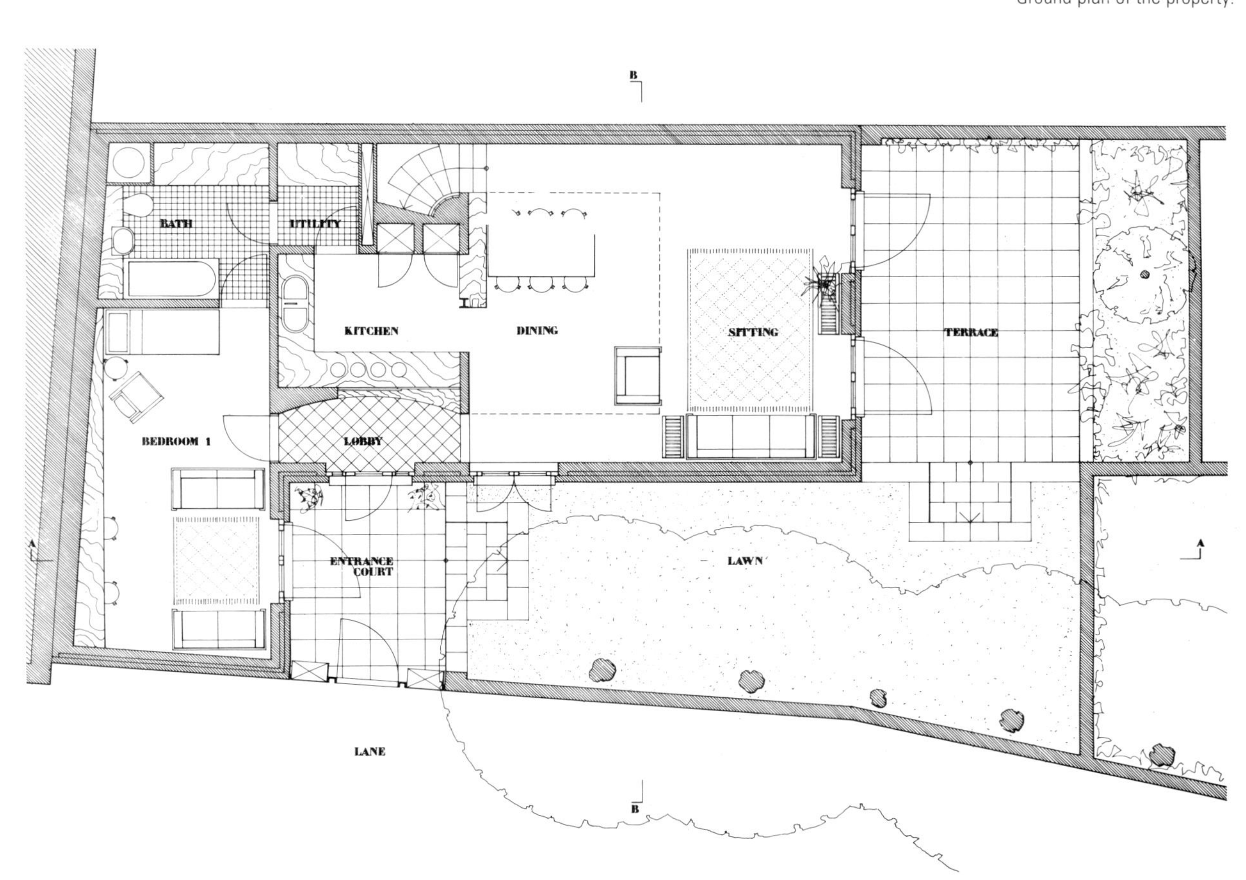

eaves and the roof could not exceed 45°. The convergence of the two modules was developed with a peaked roof, which is the highest point of the building and was utilized to increase its volumetric capacity.

The lower sections of the house are executed in brick, influenced by the typology of the surroundings, and in harmony with the old perimeter walls. Visually, several longitudinal bands of Welsh white stone vertically reorganize the building. The upper sections are finished in white stucco, establishing an abstract order with the white stone bands and with the triangular windows, whose shapes were dictated to a certain extent by the form of the slate roof. These openings are a highly expressive aesthetic motif and generate a dramatic dialogue between light and shadow.

The interior is determined by the configuration of the structure. The distribution is governed by the L-shape of the ground plan and by the different levels, as well as by the connection between the interior and the exterior. The entrance to the grounds is through a strong metal door on College Lane that opens onto the main courtyard. The ground plan is divided into two sections of different proportions that favour the division of areas. The larger section is perpendicular to the Victorian house, while the smaller one is parallel to it. The former accommodates the communal living space (the living room and the dining room) and the latter contains the rooms requiring greater privacy. At the convergence of the two modules are the service rooms (the kitchen and the toilets) and the vertical communications systems.

The dining room, staircase and gallery; the traditional concept of separate levels ceases to apply.

Plan of the upper level of the house.

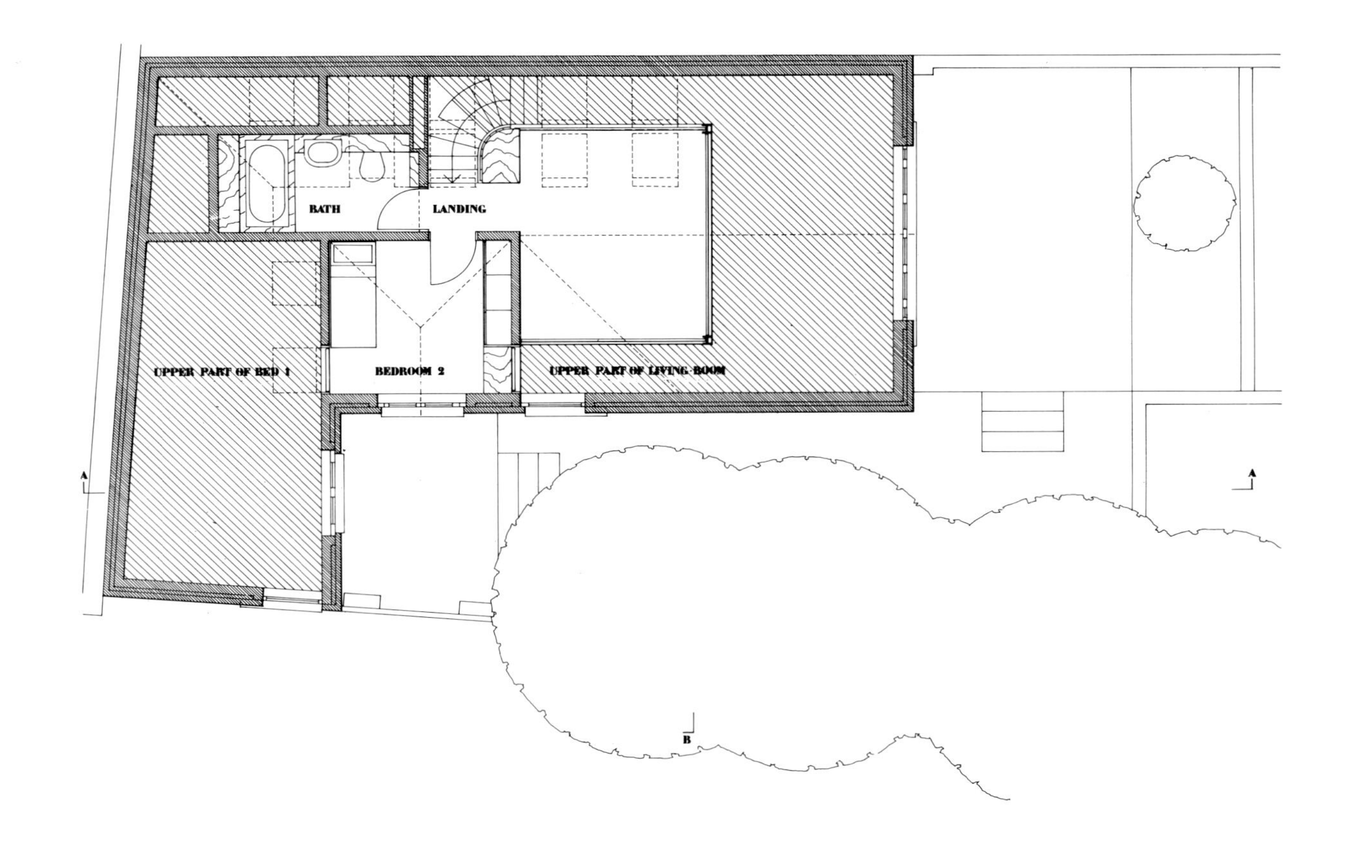

The side of the house provides ample natural light for both levels, seen here from the top of the stairs.

The programme is distributed on two basic levels. The lower level accommodates the room distribution described above. Overhead is an independent platform with no visible supports, which provides the living room with additional height and also contains a small bedroom and bath. To connect the two levels, there is a staircase against the rear wall that describes an elegant 90° helicoidal curve. The unusual distance between each of its eleven steps (210 mm) lends the structure a unique visual proportion.

The nature of Goalen's architectural achievements in planning this house was a decisive influence on the composition, distribution and decoration of the interior. The importance given to the factors of light, colour, and the economical use of space resulted in the

The staircase rises from one corner of the dining room, with its Le Corbusier-style chairs.

development of components that are highly effective both visually and pragmatically, such as the large square and triangular windows, the suspended gallery and the solutions of the roofs. The entire design reflects the influence of the rational abstract theories propounded by Le Corbusier, particularly in the severity of its lines, its formal rigor and the purity of the chromatic treatment.

The main entrance is situated on the College Lane facade, and it provides access to the foyer, characterized by an elegant curving wall, which opens in the centre, both separating and communicating with the kitchen. Its treatment in soft blue is one of the few chromatic touches in the interior built structures. The curvature and the colour combine to offer a warm welcome to the visitor, who still has no concept of the rigorous, geometric vocabulary expressed in the rest of the house. This initial space leads to the two most arresting areas: the bedroom and the living room.

The latter, designed as a studio for both work and leisure, is the largest room in the house, and above it is the startling suspended platform that organizes and distributes the different areas on this level. The living room proper is a two-storey space, while the dining room table is positioned beneath the floor slab, separated from the kitchen by a low wall with wooden shelf. The flooring is also executed in wood, in a soft shade that harmonizes perfectly with the extreme whiteness of the interior, in which only the furniture deviates from the monochromatic treatment.

The geometrical severity of the windows on the side of the house constitutes an active part of the design.

View from inside the kitchen through the dining/sitting room and out on to the terrace.

From the raised gallery the architect at his drawing table enjoys a sense of space.

View up into the gallery; the skylights are an indication of the high priority natural light occupied in the design.

Striking features of this area are the severe Le Corbusier chairs, couches and chaise longue, and a work table designed by Alvar Aalto (as is the dining room furniture). However, the most expressive effects in the interior are achieved through the magnificent natural lighting, which enters through strategically placed openings, providing the entire module with an exquisite transparency. The most aesthetic design is the wall opening onto the terrace with rectangular French doors and a large triangular window above them. The pure, clean geometry is accentuated by a very wide square grill. The orthogonal meeting of wood and glass contributes to this abstract, rational composition.

Also notable is a series of parallel openings distributed on the roof that provide direct lighting for the upper platform. The contrast of light and shade, which undergo continual change, is a highly elegant interior referent. The form of the suspended gallery makes it appear weightless, an impression reinforced by the delicate metal railing, which offers only symbolic safety. From this raised surface, the best views of the exterior can be enjoyed, as well as the luminosity that is the true protagonist of the design.

The rest of the rooms share the characteristics expressed in this main area. The master bedroom is also double height, while the small bedroom on the upper level is situated above the service area (the kitchen and the bathroom). Both are favoured by a highly rigorous geometric vocabulary and enjoy strong natural light from the exterior. The master bedroom, located in the smaller module, includes a sitting area facing the entrance courtyard. Considered as a whole, the extreme whiteness of the structures and the severity of the lines form the overall setting of a house in which light and transparency is the most significant aspect.

With this studio/residence, the architect Martin Goalen has realized a work that is a perfect combination of exterior architectural achievements and the pragmatic and aesthetic fulfillment of interior requirements. The rapport with the setting is established both physically and typologically, and the volumetric solutions (the two volumes converging at a right angle and the peaked roofs) form a group of exterior areas on different levels that contribute to the quality of the interior ambience.

The interior, based on a rigorous, abstract language drawn from the rationalism of Le Corbusier, achieves its most striking triumphs through the unusual sources of natural light, the severity and logic of the lines and the clean simplicity of the structures.

View across the sitting room; a partition wall separates th s room from the entrance lobby.